Policy Issues and Research Opportunities
in Industrial Organization

NATIONAL BUREAU OF ECONOMIC RESEARCH

General Series 96

Economic Research: Retrospect and Prospect

Policy Issues
and Research Opportunities
in Industrial Organization

Fiftieth Anniversary Colloquium III

Edited by

VICTOR R. FUCHS

National Bureau of Economic Research

NATIONAL BUREAU OF ECONOMIC RESEARCH
NEW YORK 1972

Distributed by COLUMBIA UNIVERSITY PRESS
NEW YORK AND LONDON

Relation of National Bureau Directors to Publications
Reporting Proceedings of the Fiftieth Anniversary Colloquia

Since the present volume is a record of colloquium proceedings, it has
been exempted from the rules governing submission of manuscripts to,
and critical review by, the Board of Directors of the National Bureau.
(Resolution adopted July 6, 1948, as revised
November 21, 1949, and April 20, 1968)

Prefatory Note

This volume of the Fiftieth Anniversary Series contains papers presented at the Roundtable on Policy Issues and Research Opportunities in Industrial Organization held at the University of Chicago on November 5, 1970. We are indebted to the members of the Bureau's Board of Directors who served on the committee to plan and coordinate the industrial organization session: Joseph A. Beirne, Robert A. Charpie, Nathaniel Goldfinger, Lloyd G. Reynolds, Murray Shields, George Soule, Thomas A. Wilson, and Theodore O. Yntema; and to Virginia Meltzer, Ester Moskowitz, and Ruth Ridler, who prepared the manuscript for publication.

Finally, it is with great pleasure that we dedicate this volume to Professor George J. Stigler, a pioneer in theoretical and empirical studies of industrial organization and a valued member of the National Bureau's senior research staff since 1943. His generous advice and assistance contributed substantially to the success of the roundtable session.

VICTOR R. FUCHS

Fiftieth Anniversary Colloquium and Publication Series

To commemorate its fiftieth anniversary the National Bureau of Economic Research sponsored a series of colloquia to explore the effects of pending and anticipated policy issues on future research priorities for areas of long-standing Bureau concern. As a basis for the panel and audience discussions, economists specializing in the subject area prepared papers in which they reviewed relevant research advances through time and presented their opinions for the direction of future effort. These papers, and in some instances edited transcripts of panelists' comments, appear as part of the National Bureau's Fiftieth Anniversary publications series. Papers developed for the colloquia and publications series and participants in the program included:

THE BUSINESS CYCLE TODAY
September 24, 1970—New York City

Moderators:
    Morning session: Paul A. Samuelson
    Afternoon session: F. Thomas Juster

Presentations:
    "Dating American Growth Cycles"   *Ilse Mintz*
    "The 'Recession' of 1969–1970"   *Solomon Fabricant*
    "The Cyclical Behavior of Prices"   *Geoffrey H. Moore*
    "Forecasting Economic Conditions: The Record and the Prospect"
                                         Victor Zarnowitz
    "Econometric Model Simulations and the Cyclical Characteristics
       of the U.S. Economy"   *Victor Zarnowitz*
    "A Study of Discretionary and Nondiscretionary Monetary and
       Fiscal Policies in the Context of Stochastic Macroeconometric
       Models"   *Yoel Haitovsky and Neil Wallace*

Panelists:
Morning session: Otto Eckstein, Henry C. Wallich
Afternoon session: Bert G. Hickman, Arthur M. Okun

FINANCE AND CAPITAL MARKETS
October 22, 1970—New York City

Moderator: Robert V. Roosa

Presentation:
"Finance and Capital Markets"   *John Lintner*

Panelists: William J. Baumol, Sidney Homer, James J. O'Leary

A ROUNDTABLE ON POLICY ISSUES AND RESEARCH OPPORTUNITIES IN INDUSTRIAL ORGANIZATION
November 5, 1970—Chicago, Illinois

Moderator: Victor R. Fuchs

Presentations:
"Industrial Organization: Boxing the Compass"
James W. McKie
"Antitrust Enforcement and the Modern Corporation"
Oliver E. Williamson
"Issues in the Study of Industrial Organization in a Regime of Rapid
Technical Change"   *Richard R. Nelson*
"Industrial Organization: A Proposal for Research"
Ronald H. Coase

PUBLIC EXPENDITURES AND TAXATION
December 2, 1970—Washington, D.C.

Moderator: Walter W. Heller

Presentation:
"Quantitative Research in Taxation and Government Expenditure"
Carl S. Shoup
Panelists: James M. Buchanan, Richard R. Musgrave

ECONOMIC GROWTH
December 10, 1970—San Francisco, California

Moderator: R. Aaron Gordon

Presentation:
"Is Growth Obsolete?"
William D. Nordhaus and James Tobin

Panelists: Moses Abramovitz, Robin C. O. Matthews

HUMAN RESOURCES
May 13, 1970—Atlanta, Georgia

Moderator: Gary S. Becker

Presentation:
"Human Capital: Policy Issues and Research Opportunities"
Theodore W. Schultz

Panelists: Alice M. Rivlin, Gerald S. Somers

THE FUTURE OF ECONOMIC RESEARCH
April 23, 1971—South Brookline, Massachusetts

Presentation:
"Quantitative Economic Research: Trends and Problems"

Simon Kuznets

Contents

Foreword

Whither industrial organization? That all is not well with this once flour-ishing field is readily apparent. To cite just one piece of evidence, fewer than 2 per cent of the publications in the *American Economic Review* in 1969 or 1970 were concerned with industrial organization. In former years this field accounted for at least 5 per cent of all publications.

There is nothing wrong in principle with shifts in the relative impor-tance of different research fields; indeed, a static distribution should be highly suspect. It does seem worthwhile, however, to raise a few ques-tions concerning the change. Have the problems that were formerly viewed as important all been solved? Do the problems, albeit unsolved, seem less pressing? Is current inquiry limited by the absence of new theoretical insights or by the inability to find relevant data to test these theories?

To explore these and related questions the National Bureau invited papers from four economists who have all done distinguished work in industrial organization. Their views of policy issues and research oppor-tunities have contributed substantially to the Bureau's plans for work in this field, and we are pleased to make their papers available to a wider audience. Each author makes his own distinctive contribution to the discussion, but rather than summarizing each paper I should like to identify a few common themes that run through all or most of them.

The most prominent is the call for more attention to behavior and organization *within* the firm. As Richard Nelson states it, we must go beyond the view of the firm as simply a "competent clerk" who carries out "certain well defined, widely known activities using generally avail-able resources, picking the activities and their levels according to well defined, easily computable (and optimum) decision rules."

Both Coase and Williamson stress the need to study why firms are formed and why they assume certain activities and not others. Accord-ing to Coase, "the source of the gain from having a firm is that the operation of a market costs something and that by forming an organiza-tion and allowing the allocation of resources to be determined adminis-tratively these costs are saved." In a similar vein, Williamson concludes that ". . . the question of organizational design is intrinsically interesting and inseparably associated with efficiency considerations. . . . The study of firm and market structures . . . can benefit from a more systematic examination of the sources and consequences of market failure and by a fair assessment of the powers and limits of internal organization."

A second theme, closely related to the first, is the need to define industrial organization broadly to include all kinds of organizations that use scarce resources to satisfy competing wants. Thus we are urged to pay more attention to public sector activities, nonprofit organizations, and presumably even household production. I find this emphasis particularly welcome, because, as I understand the matter, the distribution of productive activities (by type of organization) is much influenced by public policy, but economists have no theory to explain the observed distribution, to explain differences over time or space, or to predict the consequences of changes in the distribution.

A third subject that receives repeated emphasis is technological and organizational change. McKie notes that the ". . . simple equivalence of marginal cost and marginal social return is the test of welfare that we apply to practically every other allocation of resources; yet we are not remotely able to apply it at the present time to technological progress, which is itself an organic change in the use of resources." Nelson states flatly, "I do not think that the traditional theory of the firm is adequate for analysis of industries in which technical change is important"; and Williamson writes, "If one of the most remarkable attributes of American capitalism is its adaptive capacity to invent efficient viable organization forms in response to changing technological, market, and organizational conditions, to characterize the system in conventional industry terms to the neglect of internal organization easily misses much of what accounts for its most significant accomplishments."

There are, to be sure, significant differences in emphases among the papers as well as points of similarity. Williamson sees many interesting research opportunities arising out of the need to guide antitrust and regulatory policy, while Coase argues that at this stage research will proceed best in an atmosphere not directly related to policy issues. Both Nelson and Williamson appear to believe that a satisfactory theoretical framework is available; Coase, on the other hand, urges wide-ranging empirical studies on the grounds that "it is unlikely that we shall see significant advances in our theory of the organization of industry until we know more about what it is that we must explain."

Whether they are agreeing or disagreeing, however, all four authors make their points crisply and provocatively. The papers, though brief, reflect their long and varied research experience, and should prove of great interest to economists in a variety of settings—academic, business and government.

VICTOR R. FUCHS
Vice President-Research

Policy Issues and Research Opportunities
in Industrial Organization

Industrial Organization: Boxing the Compass

James W. McKie
Vanderbilt University and The Brookings Institution

Industrial organization has always prided itself on its good relation with reality. Its mission is to apply to the facts the apparatus of microeconomic theory developed by modelbuilders and systematic theoreticians. It is concerned with policy, at least to the extent of providing the best thought and analysis of economists to those who make policy. In its widest focus it is concerned with the efficiency of the arrangements, organizations, and institutions that men rely on to guide the production of what they need.

Changes in the field of industrial organization, therefore, may come in two general ways: (1) changes in the methods and tools of economic theory, which open up new paths of application; (2) changes in the real problems that men deem to be important, arising from the evolution of economic organization and from changes in the norms by which people evaluate the performance of the economy.

The contemporary state of the subject illustrates both of these influences. The newer interests are best observed against the background of the older formulation of the field, which has persisted for over 30 years and which still presents not only recurring policy issues but innumerable problems for research.

INDUSTRIAL ORGANIZATION AS A SPECIALIST SUBJECT: THE TRADITIONAL VIEW

The "tradition" is not very old; it was generated by the great upsurge of theoretical interest at the beginning of the 1930's in the economics of the firm and of imperfectly competitive markets, represented by E. H. Chamberlin [5], Joan Robinson [19], and their successors. By the end of that decade its general approach was set [14]. To be brief, it consisted of an investigation of four main aspects of the firm and the market (as well as some side issues):

1. Structure, or the relatively fixed aspects of the market environment that are not easily changed by short-run business decisions. The basic elements of market structure include the number and size distribution of sellers and buyers, the conditions of entry into the industry, demand conditions (elastic or inelastic, etc.) and the nature of the product (differentiated or homogeneous, etc.), cost conditions and technology, and influences of labor and material markets and locational factors such as transportation costs.

2. Conduct, or the behavior of firms in the market, ranging from purely competitive or price-taking behavior by firms constrained by atomistic structural conditions, to the typical maximizing behavior of a single monopolist. The types of behavior of greatest interest to specialists in industrial organization are, of course, those of oligopoly, or competition among the few.

3. Performance, or the evaluation of the results observed in the market. The most commonly used test of performance is the rate of profit (deviations in either direction too far from the norm indicate poor performance). But there are others—the size of selling costs in relation to other opportunities for competitive performance, the flexibility of prices in relation to costs, the propensity to innovate, to adopt improvements in technology, and to pass the benefits along to buyers, and the responsiveness of investment flows to profit opportunities.

4. Norms. These are the ultimate values by which the performance of firms, industries, markets, or the entire economy is judged. The most commonly recognized norms are: *efficiency* in the allocation of resources, including efficiency in minimizing costs of production; *progressiveness* in technology and organization; *equity* in income distribution and the protection of legitimate rights of various groups in the economic process; and *stability* of employment, incomes, and prices. These various norms may conflict with each other, at least in part, which in turn can lead to inconsistencies in the public policies that are responsive to them. The conflict between efficiency and equity as norms of performance in economic organization has become especially noteworthy in recent times.

Research in industrial organization has not—or not yet—succeeded in constructing a completely connected system linking together these four aspects in an articulated reversible scheme for analysis and policy. Besides producing a great deal of research on particular facets of structure and types of behavior, it has established links between structure and *performance* (as judged by certain norms) and has constructed some generalizations on the relationship between structure and *behavior* in particular markets of the modern industrial state.

Investigations of economic performance usually bypass behavioral problems and go directly to the configurations of market structure that tend to produce adequate (or good) performance—generally judged by the norm of allocative efficiency, since different norms may produce different conclusions about structure. This inquiry makes use of a variety of equilibrium models of the market. It usually relies on the purely competitive model as an "ideal" of efficient resource allocation. The relation between market structure and profit performance has been extensively researched.[1] Less is known about the relation between market structure and other norms—notably progressiveness—and hardly anything about the effect of market structure on aggregate (macroeconomic) stability. These are important issues, and we should continue to try to learn more about the relationships.

Besides the approach to performance there is the approach to behavior. I have argued elsewhere [15] that insufficient attention has been given to this kind of analysis—essentially positivist rather than normative. Perhaps it has had less appeal to economists because of their preoccupation with equilibrium solutions and with the efficiency norm. Behavioral analysis is concerned less with an evaluation of an equilibrium result than with an ongoing process and its structural determinants. It is a particularly interesting approach in oligopoly markets, which show such marked deviations from simple equilibrium and such a wide dispersion of behavior patterns.

Economic analysis has made some progress in predicting patterns of behavior (conduct) in various kinds of markets, both oligopolistic and nonoligopolistic, from certain combinations of structural elements. We know, for example, what configurations of structure are likely to produce basing-point systems; strong price leadership; chronic price warfare; market sharing; and that pattern of disorderly competition that has come to be known as the "cartel syndrome." There is always some danger of anecdotal explanations and ad hoc analysis in this approach. Nevertheless I think we need to carry it much farther, with the aid of new tools of analysis. We have some obligation as economists to explain the economic behavior that we observe, even though at present we can't link up most behavior patterns with definite evaluations of performance.

[1] [2, 3, 6, 11, 23], for example.

Economic explanations of behavior have not yet made full use of organization theory—that is, the behavioral theory of the firm and its analysis as a functioning organism. Economists have usually assumed that the firm is a single decisionmaking unit motivated entirely by the desire for maximum profits—and for many purposes of economic analysis nothing more is needed. But for analysis of behavior, particularly in the oligopolistic markets where large firms have relatively wide options and face a complex set of constraints, an amalgam of organization and market theory should be fruitful.[2] The pioneering work of Oliver Williamson [28], William Baumol [4], and other scholars [3] should be pushed along (and no doubt will be, by them and by others) until we can incorporate managerial economics and market analysis into the same system, with common axioms and analytical structure.

Pushing back the frontiers of the major problems of industrial organization does not reduce the need for continued spadework in the "old" areas. The need for factual input is enormous. The underlying structure evolves, and our bank of information needs to be kept up to date. New forms of organization appear, and the changes must be evaluated, trends projected, effects of new technology predicted, and changes in concentration and integration charted. Even such an old-fashioned form as the traditional "industry study" fills a continuing need. Without a continuous renewal of our fund of factual material and structural analysis in the basic categories of industrial organization, the more advanced applications of the subject would eventually wither.

Other Research in the Familiar Directions

A considerable amount of research effort has been devoted to certain issues in industrial organization without producing final, or even semifinal, answers that are satisfactory in the present milieu. The deficiencies are partly due to the continued evolution of the problems. In any case, more research is called for. Several examples follow.

1. Structure and Equity.   For many years we have witnessed the growing influence of equity on public policy and market organiza-

---

[2] There is no good evidence that maximum profits as a goal of the enterprise have been superseded by a managerial "utility function in five variables" (Adelman [1], p. 137). But profit maximizing does not necessarily lead to a predictable equilibrium in oligopoly markets, nor does the goal explain the process of reaching it.

[3] Not forgetting the contributions from the direction of managerial science by Cyert and March [7] and many others.

tion. Economists, wedded to the norm of allocative efficiency, have generally taken an unfavorable view of this trend. We have been prone to view equity as a matter of the distribution of income, and economic theory tells us that distributive considerations need not interfere with efficiency in resource allocation. Once the economy meets the optimum conditions for allocation, any distributive shortcoming can be met by direct redistribution. There are no problems that can't be solved by paying someone a lump sum or collecting a lump sum from him.

Public officials and policymakers have shown little interest in this prescription for a solution of the equity problems, nor have they found the political means by which direct income transfers could substitute for other policies responsive to problems of equity. Instead, public policy has frequently chosen to change market structure to deal with those problems. It has, in other words, created or fostered or protected monopoly and organizational power to correct what was thought to be a disadvantageous income position for certain groups. It has also done this to protect other kinds of equitable rights. We used to call this the "drift toward Syndicalism," though now we might call it the evolution of the New Industrial State or perhaps the Emerging Tribe. The government has not only conferred economic power upon groups to further their own interests but has inevitably become involved in guiding the relationships and settling disputes among these power blocs.

Both the rationalization and the consequences of such policies remain obscure. Public authorities often claim to be moved by the inferior "bargaining power" of certain groups to confer monopoly powers upon them; yet the true economic basis of inferior bargaining power (which must be related to market structure) has not been adequately investigated nor demonstrated—nor have the effects of these policies upon economic efficiency. Public policy seems to have undertaken a great many individual alterations of market organization for the sake of equity without even a partial-equilibrium prediction of the economic effects, let alone of the consequences for the over-all configuration of the market system. If the phenomenon is largely political or sociological, we are again faced with the imperative necessity of working in the interdisciplinary fields and approaching somewhat closer to a unified social science—or at least to a dialogue with the other disciplines, which also have their explanations and predictions of the newly emerging forms of organization.[4]

[4] If the free market were to be replaced entirely by direct negotiations and quasi-political relations among organized groups, much of the economic theory of

2. The Economics of Technological Change.   It may appear impertinent for anyone to suggest that more work remains to be done on the economics of technological change, in view of the major book-length studies that have recently appeared [5] and the countless articles in the professional journals during the last few decades. This work has undoubtedly greatly increased our knowledge. On some phases of the matter it has provided at least tentative answers to formerly puzzling questions, such as: do the degrees of monopoly and inventiveness show a positive correlation; are the most monopolistic firms the most inventive; and do the largest firms in technologically advanced industries typically introduce most of the innovations? We are reasonably sure now that the relation between market power and inventiveness (or progressiveness) is not monotonic, though we are less sure of where the maximum is. We know also that other variables affect the relationship strongly. Further research might give policymakers the ability to fine-tune the relationship between patent protection, for instance, and some target rate of technological change in the economy, by altering the structure of inducements to innovate and eliminating the "rents" or unnecessary returns.

Behind these questions, however, lurk others—vastly important, and even farther from solution. One is the problem of determining the optimum rate of technological change itself. To arrive at an estimate of a target rate we would need to know three things that we do not know now: (1) how to measure all of the effects of technological change, both direct and indirect, in an immensely complex web of social interconnections—i.e., "technological evaluation" in economic terms; (2) how to translate social values and norms, both economic and noneconomic, into operationally applicable measures of social benefit and social harm; (3) how to compare the marginal social cost of a technological change, including the inefficiencies of allocation in the static sense that may be necessary to induce innovation, with the marginal social benefits of the change. This simple equivalence of marginal cost and marginal social return is the test of welfare that we apply to practically every other allocation of resources, yet we are not remotely able to apply it at the present time to technological progress, which is itself an organic change in the use of resources.[6]

the market would require transmutation, to a theory of group bargaining or multilateral monopoly with a tincture of "countervailing power."

[5] [12, 13, 16, 17, 20], to name some outstanding examples.

[6] Uncertainty has been an impenetrable barrier to *ex ante* evaluation of invention and innovation. The noteworthy progress in the theory of risk and uncer-

The normative nature of the problem has to be recognized. A survey of the literature reveals an extraordinarily uncritical acceptance of a naive formulation of progress as a norm: it is "good"; so good that faster is always better; so good that any amount of technological progress, no matter how small, is worth any cost in terms of present distortion of allocative efficiency, no matter how large; so good that all of the side effects can be ignored. What we must do is work out the tradeoffs against which to make normative choices, and analyze the externalities and organizational impact of technology to a degree never before attempted. Other branches of economics are involved in this research—notably welfare economics, which faces a peculiarly difficult task in analyzing a dynamic process in which both preferences and the means of satisfying them are changing. But industrial organization should try to attain a better understanding of the complex interactions between innovation and market structure.

In addition to the suggested research on factor combinations and market performance in technological change, we need better models of the firm as an innovating mechanism. Invention innovation is a *process* (whether creative or destructive in its ultimate effects) working through an institutional structure.[7] It seems to be partly volitional, partly adaptive, partly stochastic. We also need better understanding of the natural selection of successful innovation in the economic environment. These are problems for social science, not for economics alone.

3. Regulatory Policy.   Research on the old-line policy questions keeps regenerating itself because the problems keep regenerating themselves. Specialists in the field, both lawyers and economists, well know the delights of analyzing particular antitrust cases, at least the big ones, which present a never-repeating kaleidoscope of variations in economic facts and policy questions. But a somewhat more systematic effort is required for the formulation of general policy, even after all this time. The most recent general formulations of economic standards for antitrust policy—the reports of the so-called Neal [25] and Stigler [27] task forces—show how much still needs to be done.

tainty needs to be applied more searchingly to the economics of innovation to see whether it will help to break the uncertainty barrier.

[7] R. A. Solo in a recent review [23] of the Mansfield volumes calls for a framework for analysis that can "contain the generation, recapitulation, dissemination of information, the determinants of creativity, the process of learning by individuals and groups, . . . the receptivity or resistance to novelty" and other elements of the process of technological change.

The recommendations in the "Neal Report" for deconcentration of concentrated industries were based on economic research (which was not available to the Attorney General's Committee of the 1950's [26]) that indicated that economic performance in oligopoly tends to become distinctly unsatisfactory when the concentration rises above a critical zone and when certain other structural conditions are present, such as blockaded entry. These findings provide empirical reinforcement for a longstanding public antipathy to economic concentration and market power —an attitude supported, though somewhat gingerly, by the antitrust laws. It is fair to say that economic research has not reached a position of certainty on the relations between structure and performance.[8] It cannot yet give public policy entirely reliable guidance on every question that arises in connection with industry structure and market behavior. I need only mention as an illustrative case the enigma of advertising as a barrier to entry.

For the present, no policy of drastic modification of existing industry structure in the U.S. appears likely. The only active questions of structural change right now are those involving mergers and conglomerate firms. In the case of the large conglomerate, our theory of the firm is clearly inadequate to enable us to understand its nature or predict its performance—more or less necessary prerequisites for advice to policy-makers—though the combined trends in concentration and growth of conglomerates into concentrated markets is sufficient cause for concern. Research scholars have lately shown a very active interest in the conglomerate organization, demonstrated by the volume of publications on conglomerate mergers.

Externalities, or the effects of activity by one organization or industry upon others, is another aspect of industrial organization on which research has taken a sudden upsurge. Few questions have elicited so much popular interest in recent times as externalities, especially those that fit under the rubrics of "pollution" and "conservation." Professional interest has reacted similarly. I shall have more to say about this direction of research a little further on.

The effort to bring externalities under public control is merely one aspect of a major proliferation of government controls and "policies" on economic organization, abetted by what might be called the atrophy of laissez-faire and loss of belief in the ability of a free economy to run

[8] Eugene M. Singer [22] says that the Neal Report shows "how far an elementary structural approach can be carried in public policy."

itself. It was formerly agreed, on the whole, that the government need intervene only in those cases where the market failed to work, and failed in an egregious manner. But one no longer hears of the dichotomy of the public utilities and the others. The public utility industry is merely one of a constellation of types which are all "regulated" in some degree, or which at least encounter government policies shaped to fit their micro-economic structure. The predominant attitude among the public, if not among economists, is that public policy—regulatory, monitory, corrective, or protective—is normally needed in most activities, and that we probably don't have enough of it.

Economists who specialize in industrial organization have tried to be of use in this climate of opinion, though sometimes without much enthusiasm. Interest in regulation and regulatory problems has burgeoned. Economists have offered and will offer a great deal of advice to public officials on how to put regulation on a sound economic footing. They have studied market failure in many industries, and recommended new forms of policy to deal with it. They have even studied the problem of limits to effective regulation and what might be called the flaws in the regulatory solution to market imperfections.[9] Given the current drift in attitudes toward political economy, the increasing complexity and interdependence of economic activity, and the proliferation of problems that the market does not seem able to cope with effectively, this research interest is bound to intensify. It deserves support, since better understanding of the relationship of regulation to industrial organization will probably have a high payoff in the avoidance of gross errors of public policy. (Of course, one can find examples on both sides of this proposition.)

The New Industrial Organization

In the preface to his recent brilliant text on industrial organization, William G. Shepherd says:

> Some years ago, a senior colleague advised me that research on market structure was mostly "wrapped up and done." Soon thereafter another and younger friend, now a well-known specialist in the field, urged upon me that the "old" industrial organization

[9] All of these research interests are exemplified in the current program of Studies in the Regulation of Economic Activity of The Brookings Institution, as well as in other research programs.

field—by which he meant the issues which are covered in this book
—was "dead." [10]

Shepherd's own book is conclusive testimony to the contrary, but
one is led to speculate on what the younger colleague had in mind. Was
there a "new" industrial organization that was alive and growing? Perhaps not; but if there was, it was probably to be an econometric or
statistical one.

The intensive application of quantitative methods in all branches of
economics shows no signs of diminishing—indeed, most fledgling economists now seem to win their wings this way—but there may be a little
less optimism than formerly about its ability to clarify outstanding difficulties in economics. In industrial organization, quantitative research has
been applied chiefly to testing the relationship between industry structure and various dimensions of performance—an "old" problem. This
has been moderately illuminating. So has the simulation and statistical
testing of theorems about market behavior. The old squabbles about
rational behavior and the logical consequences of assumptions about
market structure do not seem to have been solved empirically, however:
they have been transmuted into squabbles about correspondence, identi-
fication, reliability of data, structure of equations, parameters, and statistical significance. Perhaps the greatest value that statistical testing has
for the research scholar (as opposed to the policymaker) is to send him
back to the drawing board repeatedly to see whether his theory and the
hypotheses drawn from it can't be improved.[11]

Besides testing the implications of market theory, quantitative
research has turned its attention to measuring various attributes of business behavior and the productive structure of the firm. Some of this has
been quite useful, though it must be said that some appears to have been
undertaken merely because the tools of measurement were available and
someone wanted to try them out. Repetitive measurements and statistical

[10] [21], p. v. For other pessimistic views, see [9, 10, 22].

[11] Shepherd [21] notes, "To those willing to believe that if one cannot measure
X on the first try, then X doesn't exist, the scattered empirical findings have made
it possible to 'show' that concentration is inconsequential" (pp. 21–22). Also:
"The rush to 'test' concepts empirically has degenerated frequently into a sort of
scientism, in which a lack of findings in a faulty test using slender evidence was
asserted to disprove the existence of otherwise likely phenomena" (p. 23). Grabowski and Mueller [9], p. 100, further assert that "we stand in the danger of
seeing the period of infancy in the application of econometrics to industrial
organization coincide with its zenith, unless we are able to develop better theories
and/or come up with better data than are presently available."

formulations of endless varieties of production functions, for example, go into the data bank as building blocks for future systematic formulations on a theoretical foundation. Building blocks are useful, even essential, things to have, as long as we don't use them to build the Tower of Babel.

THE NEW, NEW INDUSTRIAL ORGANIZATION

Earlier in this survey I referred to several "familiar" directions of research in industrial organization—including (1) concern with problems of equity and distribution; (2) concern with evaluating the causes and consequences of technological change; (3) concern with external costs and benefits which escape accounting and evaluation in existing market organization; (4) concern with the public role in economic life and its tendency to enlarge itself as people become dissatisfied with the results of free, uncontrolled markets. The quantitative methods mentioned above have created some new and refined tools for this research but they do not in themselves change its meaning.

But if we push these concerns far enough, we leave the familiar territory of industrial organization—in truth, of orthodox economics itself—and sail beyond the edge of the charts. We have long known that those regions were out there, but with a kind of notional assent not involving systematic professional research interest. Now, however, the problems beckon.

The swell of discontent with our industrial society, its institutions, and its organizations is reaching such proportions that economists who concern themeselves with "organization" must soon decide whether they are going to participate in this debate or to disdain the whole matter as an unscientific uproar created by an undisciplined rabble. If we decide to ignore it we run some risk of losing "relevance" to the problems that vast numbers of our students and other fellow citizens think are important. Yet it is admittedly difficult for an "orthodox" economist to make much sense out of this uproar or to use his battery of analytic tools, as they exist now, to carve out solutions. It is no wonder that most of my colleagues regard this newest wave with mingled puzzlement and exasperation. Even those who participate in it seem to leave their scientific apparatus behind in the classrooms and laboratories as they run out to join the mobs on the quad.

The extreme view, being disorderly, cannot be summed up in a single formulation. It is not all new, since it contains many fragments of old socialism ranging from the Marxist to the Utopian. So far as one can discern the form of its basic attitudes on economics through the burning haze of its rhetoric, they seem to be about as follows. Most "goods" are actually bads, not produced to satisfy any fundamental human needs or wants, and forced on an apathetic populace by a greedy and irresponsible group of giant corporations. This view denies the primacy of wants. Consumer behavior in the marketplace is said to be the result of manipulation. Satisfaction of wants is illusory.[12] Self-interest is thought to be equivalent to greed and to the intent to exploit others; the invisible hand is a myth; the enterprise system in the "free market" is actually an engine which encourages and facilitates the exploitation of some groups by others. A variant of this view is that industry or the "corporate state" are altogether out of human control, having made unwitting captives of the people who are supposed to own and direct it. Technology has become self-directed, and the corporate state in both its industrial and governmental aspects is completely unresponsive to human needs.

The new-radical view of human nature (from which "economic man" has been expelled) is, of course, Rousseauist, in contrast to the Hobbesian view that most orthodox economists over thirty come to when they go behind the symbols and axioms to the substance of behavior and motivation. It follows that the rebels want to make interpersonal comparisons the very basis of public policy. In their view, human beings (and maybe other species too) are absolutely equal, and apparently are to have common rights in all attributes and usufructs of social organization, not excepting the economy.

Strong views, these, and very hard words. What should we make of them? I will leave it to others to deal with the welfare and behavioral aspects of the new wave, and consider what might result for research in "industrial organization" if we take it seriously.

To use the conventional language of economics, one major concern of the critics is with externalities. It would be wrong to say that economists have not been concerned with externalities; there is a voluminous literature defining them, analyzing their origins, and deducing their welfare implications. Activities generating external benefits (scientific re-

---

[12] As Charles Reich expressed this view in a recent article [18], "Advertising is designed to create, and does create, dissatisfaction. But dissatisfaction is no mere toy. If one creates a desire for sex, status, and excitement, and then sells a man an automobile, the desire is likely to remain unsatisfied. The wants created are real enough, but the satisfactions are unreal" (p. 89).

search, education, landscaping) and external costs (rendering plants, dilapidated housing, commercial fishing) are well-known. What is new is the enormous increase both in the scope of externalities and in public awareness of them.

Economists should increase their own contribution to knowledge of these phenomena; they have already begun to do so. I do not say that our analysis will lead to the point where we can write down a single production function for the whole economic system. But such research would in all probability increase our awareness of the interdependence of economic activity along with providing the rest of the world with a more accurate picture of what the interrelationships, costs, and benefits really are.[13] Industrial organization is necessarily involved in research on externalities because of the industrial locus of much of the problem and because any rational solutions are likely to require policies that alter the workings of certain markets—perhaps of most markets. These solutions may not satisfy all of the critics, of course, but then economics is not an apocalyptic discipline.

Similar efforts are called for on the other matters mentioned above. Ultimately, specialists in industrial organization may be expected to answer the question of whether large, bureaucratic organizations staffed by specialists are necessary in industry and government to make an economy based on an advanced technology work with tolerable efficiency; [14] or, if some other set of goals is advanced as an alternative to the ones that have guided Western economic growth for two centuries, to determine what the consequences might be for the organization of production and distribution. If we are really in a process of change from an extensive, waste-making, progressive, space-using, technologically oriented society toward an intensive, conserving, relatively static society oriented primarily toward equity and the needs of social participation, the implications for industrial organization will be profound. All agencies of economic and social research will be called on to participate in solving the problems.

[13] For a laboratory exercise, we might consider the true costs and benefits of energy production and use in the United States.
[14] Similar questions are often asked by other analysts who do not necessarily share the attitudes of the "new-radical" critics: cf. Galbraith [8].

REFERENCES

1. Adelman, M. A., " 'World Oil' and the Theory of Industrial Organization," in Jesse W. Markham, ed., *Industrial Organization and Economic Development,* Boston, Houghton Mifflin, 1970.
2. Bain, Joe S., *Barriers to New Competition,* Cambridge, Harvard University Press, 1956.
3. ———, *Industrial Organization,* 2d edition, New York, John Wiley & Sons, Inc., 1968.
4. Baumol, William J., *Economic Theory and Operations Analysis,* rev. ed., Englewood Cliffs, N.J., Prentice-Hall, Inc., 1966.
5. Chamberlin, Edward H., *The Theory of Monopolistic Competition,* Cambridge, Harvard University Press, 1933.
6. Collins, N. R., and Preston, Lee E., "Price-Cost Margins and Industry Structure," *Review of Economics and Statistics,* August 1969.
7. Cyert, Richard M., and March, James G., *A Behavioral Theory of the Firm,* Englewood Cliffs, N.J., Prentice-Hall, Inc., 1963.
8. Galbraith, John Kenneth, *The New Industrial State,* Boston, Houghton Mifflin, 1967.
9. Grabowski, Henry, and Mueller, Dennis, "Industrial Organization: The Role and Contribution of Econometrics," *American Economic Review,* May 1970.
10. Grether, E. T., "Industrial Organization: Past History and Future Problems," *American Economic Review,* May 1970.
11. Mann, H. Michael, "Seller Concentration, Barriers to Entry, and Rates of Return in Thirty Industries, 1950–1960," *Review of Economics and Statistics,* August 1966.
12. Mansfield, Edwin, *The Economics of Technological Change,* New York, W. W. Norton, 1968.
13. ———, *Industrial Research and Technological Change,* New York, W. W. Norton, 1968.
14. Mason, Edward S., "Price and Production Policies of Large-Scale Enterprise," *American Economic Review* (supplement), March 1939.
15. McKie, James W., "Market Structure and Function: Performance and Behavior," in Jesse W. Markham, ed., *Industrial Organization and Economic Development,* Boston, Houghton Mifflin, 1970.
16. Nelson, Richard R., ed., *The Rate and Direction of Inventive Activity: Economic and Social Factors,* National Bureau of Economic Research Special Conference Series 13, Princeton University Press for NBER, 1962.
17. Nelson, Richard R., Peck, Merton J., and Kalachek, Edward, *Technology, Economic Growth and Public Policy,* Washington, The Brookings Institution, 1967.
18. Reich, Charles A., "The Greening of America," *The New Yorker,* September 26, 1970.
19. Robinson, Joan, *The Economics of Imperfect Competition,* London, The Macmillan Company, 1933.
20. Schmookler, Jacob, *Innovation and Economic Growth,* Cambridge, Harvard University Press, 1966.
21. Shepherd, William G., *Market Power and Economic Welfare,* New York, Random House, 1970.

22. Singer, Eugene M., "Industrial Organization: Price Models and Public Policy," *American Economic Review,* May 1970.
23. Solo, Robert A., "Economics of Technological Change" (Reviews), *Journal of Economic Literature,* September 1969.
24. Stigler, George J., "A Theory of Oligopoly," *Journal of Political Economy,* February 1964.
25. United States Government, *The Presidential Task Force Report on Antitrust Policy,* Washington, 1969, reprinted in *Antitrust Law and Economics Review,* Winter 1968–69.
26. ———, *Report of the U.S. Attorney General's National Committee to Study the Antitrust Laws,* Washington, 1955.
27. ———, "Task Force on Productivity and Competition," published in the *Congressional Record,* June 16, 1969, p. S6472.
28. Williamson, Oliver E., *The Economics of Discretionary Behavior: Managerial Objectives in a Theory of the Firm,* Englewood Cliffs, N.J., Prentice-Hall, Inc., 1964.

Antitrust Enforcement and the Modern Corporation

Oliver E. Williamson
University of Pennsylvania

My discussion of policy issues and research opportunities in industrial organization is principally concerned with issues where the analyses of firm and market structures overlap, with special attention to matters that fall within the ambit of antitrust enforcement. I take the position that a re-examination of the implicit assumptions of conventional firm and market models is needed if antitrust analysts are accurately to assess the properties of the modern corporation and the markets within which it operates. I suggest, in this connection, that an "institutional failures" orientation—to include an assessment of the failures of internal organization (administrative processes) as well as failures of product and capital markets—can usefully be adopted by students of antitrust economics.

Among the matters that come under review are the influence of product market failures (of both conventional and unconventional sorts) on the dominant firm condition and on vertical integration. Failures in the capital market as these relate to conglomerate organization are also examined. But no discussion of firm and market structures is complete without calling attention to the limits of internal organization. Markets, after all, do not fail absolutely, but only in relation to some nonmarket alternative (Arrow, 1969, p. 48). Focusing, as I attempt to, on the transactional relations that occur within and between firms and markets makes especially evident that internal organization and market processes can, for many purposes, usefully be regarded as substitutes.

The differences between this and the usual industrial organization approach warrant explication. It is not, I think, a caricature to say that the internal organization of the firm, including the allocation of functions between firms and markets, is of concern to traditional analysis

Note: Research on this paper has been supported by a grant from The Brookings Institution. It is part of a larger study also supported by Brookings. The opinions expressed are my own.

mainly as this can be said to influence "market power" and "offensive business conduct." By contrast, I treat the question of organizational design as intrinsically interesting and inseparably associated with efficiency considerations. Firms become devices for alleviating market frictions (failures) by internalizing activities that might otherwise be performed by the market. The limitations of firms for these purposes, while real, are a function of organization form. The study of organizational innovations, consequently, is a matter of special interest. Altogether, the approach that I am advocating is one of "transactional analysis of a comparative-institutional sort." While there is no essential conflict between this and "market power analysis" of the usual variety (indeed they ought to be regarded as complements), the research programs suggested by each are quite different.

I conclude that an incomplete treatment of the dominant firm problem in economics has led to an incorrect characterization of the monopoly problem by the law, and that antitrust has been undiscriminating in its treatment of both vertical and conglomerate structures. In more numerous respects than are generally recognized, vertical integration and conglomerate organization permit transactional failures (in the product and capital markets, respectively) to be attenuated.

I. DOMINANT FIRM INDUSTRIES

Issues

Antitrust is on its most familiar ground when dealing with conventional monopoly problems that take the form of horizontal market power. The underlying economic theory here is thought to be relatively well developed and its applications obvious. Still, neither the courts nor the enforcement agencies have been prepared seriously to challenge pre-existing market power that takes the form of a dominant firm.

As the law is currently interpreted, dominance does not constitute a Section 2 monopoly violation if the structure in question is attributable to "a superior product, business acumen, or historic accident." [1] Although, in practice, the courts may never explicitly entertain defenses to dominance along any of these lines, merely to offer them in principle has enforcement significance: the enforcement agencies are precluded from using any of these hypothetical defenses as an affirmative reason for bringing a case. That, in these circumstances, dominant firm com-

[1] United States v. Grinnell Corp., 384 U.S. 563, 571 (1966).

plaints rely mainly on alleged conduct offenses is only to be expected. This often reduces them, however, to contrived cases, and legitimate issues are suppressed.

Evaluation

Dominant firm industries will be defined, provisionally, to be industries for which the output of the dominant firm has persistently exceeded 60 per cent of the industry total. The dominant firms in such industries will ordinarily enjoy supernormal rates of return—at least potentially if not actually.[2] Two issues are especially relevant in assessing the dominant firm condition: How did dominance develop? What remedies, if any, ought to be invoked?

The usual assumption, implicit if not explicit, in most treatments of the dominant firm issue is that "competition works"—at least in the limited sense that extant and potential rivals can be relied upon to perform self-policing functions by responding appropriately to opportunities for private gain. But for circumstances in which economies of scale are large in relation to the market, patent protection exists, or illegal practices are employed, persistent dominance with monopoly returns is not to be expected. Still, reference by the Court to business acumen and historic accident defenses reveals a chink in the workability argument that just possibly warrants closer attention. Ought differential expertise and chance event effects to be regarded as manifestations of market failure, and what are the policy implications?

It is proposed here that differential expertise in amounts sufficient to support dominance be regarded as a failure in the market for managerial talent. This can take either of two forms. First, the requisite talents may simply be scarce. Thus although it is usually assumed that the supply of managerial talent is quite adequate (Kaysen and Turner, 1959, pp. 9, 117), at least occasionally this may not be true. Marschak, in a related context, puts the issue as follows: "There exist almost unique, irreplaceable research workers, teachers, administrators; just as there exist unique choice locations for plants and harbors. The problem of unique or imperfectly standardized goods . . . has been neglected by the textbooks" (1968, p. 14). The possibility that the dominant firm has gained ascendancy because of the inimitable quality of its management at least warrants consideration.

---

[2] Sometimes these firms may be run slack, in which case reported profit will not disclose the full supernormal profit potential.

This is not, however, the only possibility. The dominant firm may have displayed no special management expertise but existing and potential rivals, on which the responsibility for self-policing functions devolves, may have been uncommonly inept. Persistent ineptitude of this sort is an indication that the self-policing functions of rivalry have lapsed. Such discreditable performance on the part of principal rivals during critical formative stages of an industry's development will be referred to as *default failure*.

Whether, however, a default failure outcome is more than a hypothetical possibility—to be conceded in principle but not observed in practice—is perhaps to be doubted. Relevant in this connection is the experience of the diesel locomotive industry, where an argument not only can but has been advanced that the dominance by General Motors in diesel locomotive manufacture is to be explained by default failure among the steam locomotive firms.[3] Although this record needs to be more thoroughly developed and documented, I find the evidence more than suggestive that General Motors' dominance of this industry was the result of ineptitude on the part of the steam locomotive manufacturers and imperceptiveness among potential rivals.

Consider now the historic accident defense. Dominance that results from an unusual run of luck will be referred to as *chance event failure*. The dominant firm and its rivals may be performing in a fully creditable (yet unexceptional) manner, but the dominant firm is thrust ahead by an unusual sequence of fortuitous events.

The extensive literature on stochastic determinants of firm size is relevant in this connection. The usual and simplest assumption here is that all firms in an industry prospectively have access to identical mean growth rates, with actual rates being assigned at random from a common probability distribution. In the absence of serial correlation, a firm that experiences high growth in one period may easily "draw" a low growth rate in the next; no special advantage need obtain. Occasionally, however, a firm may enjoy an unusual run of luck; a series of supernormal growth rates are strung together. Where this happens, the lucky firm can be thrust into a position of dominance. Moreover, the dominance outcome, once realized, may not easily be undone by continued application of the same stochastic mechanism: "Once the most fortunate firms

[3] See the testimony, including exhibits, of C. R. Osborne in *A Study of the Antitrust Laws,* Hearings before the Senate Subcommittee on Antitrust and Monopoly of the Committee on the Judiciary, 84th Cong., 1st Sess., Part 8, December 9, 1955, Washington, D.C., 1956, pp. 3948–97.

climb well ahead of the pack, it is difficult for laggards to rally and rectify the imbalance, for by definition, each firm—large and small—has an equal chance of growing by an equal percentage amount" (Scherer, 1970, p. 127). If indeed the variance in growth rates declines as an industry matures and technical progress slackens, the prospect that a dominant firm outcome once established will subsequently be upset (in any short period of time) by chance market processes is correspondingly impaired.

As a policy matter, it would seem appropriate to regard both default and chance event failures that result in dominance as indications that the self-policing properties of the market, in these respects, have broken down. Intervention by the government on grounds of "residual responsibility" to restore a more competitive outcome is arguably appropriate. New bases upon which to rest a Section 2 violation that do not rely exclusively or primarily on conduct offenses would in this way become available to the enforcement agencies. Moreover, structural relief, where either default or chance event failures are established (and countervailing considerations do not obtain), is presumably warranted. Altogether, more assertive antitrust enforcement toward the dominant firm industries would emerge.

It might be noted that Turner (1969) has recently reached a similar policy conclusion concerning dominant firm industries—albeit on somewhat different grounds. Turner appeals to "reasonableness" considerations in suggesting that, but for scale economy or unexpired patent defenses, "it is appropriate to put a time limit on continuing monopoly power that rests in part on earlier success, regardless of how the early success was achieved" (p. 1219). The advantage of the present argument is that implementing such a proposal is more attractive where significant default or chance event failures can be shown to have occurred.

The position of Posner (1969, pp. 1596–98) on persistent monopoly can also be assessed in the light of the above argument. Posner objects to Section 2 dissolution proceedings as a means for dealing with persistent dominance on the grounds that monopoly positions not supported by scale economies, predatory behavior, superior skill, or forgone monopoly gains will *usually* be eliminated by market processes. One can agree, especially if the time horizon stipulated is sufficiently long. If, however, a dominant firm position, once secured, may be undone by unassisted market processes only with difficulty, a policy of waiting for self-correcting measures to be effective in a market where the dominance outcome has resulted from chance event or default failures is, perhaps, excessively passive. Unusual measures may be indicated when the unusual event obtains.[4]

Research Opportunities

However one comes out on the policy ramifications of the argument, it is a matter of scientific interest that a series of *focused* industry studies of the dominant firm industries be conducted. Can default or chance event failures reasonably be established, or is the dominant firm outcome invariably to be attributed to scale economies, unexpired original patents, or illegal conduct? The matter can be approached directly, by examining both the properties of the decisions taken by the dominant firm's principal rivals (default failure) and the stochastic experience of the industry (chance events),[5] and indirectly, by assessing the conventional scale economy, patent, and conduct conditions. But for nontrivial scale economy, patent, or conduct effects, or unless management superiority claims can be supported, default or chance event failures are presumably to be inferred. Claims of management superiority are difficult to evaluate in any simple way, but the study of organizational innovations, with special attention to changes in organization form, may sometimes permit indirect inferences to be made. [See in this connection Chandler (1966) and Williamson (1970).]

None of this requires that the relief question be reached. If, however, as a policy matter, the question of dissolution is seriously to be considered, it is further necessary to examine both the human and physical assets in the dominant firm. Should a study reveal that the requisite managerial and technical capabilities are impacted, in the sense that these cannot easily be assembled by unassisted market processes, any

[4] Posner argues elsewhere that inasmuch as "a recent study [Brozen's (1970)] found that a high level of concentration in an industry tends to dissipate by natural forces within an average period of 10 years . . . [and since] the average length of a divestiture proceeding in a monopolization case involving a major regional or national market is 8 years, . . . it seems unlikely that administrative methods of deconcentration will work significantly more rapidly than the market" (1970, p. 417, n. 50). The argument has merit but relies heavily on average market tendencies which, in the particular cases of very high concentration that we are concerned with here, may be unwarranted. It also takes prevailing judicial practices as given, despite reform proposals concerning this matter [see, for example, the Neale Task Force Report (1969)].

[5] Examination of unanticipated technical and market developments as well as product life cycle effects are relevant to an assessment of chance event failures.

dissolution effort ought presumably to attempt to transfer human as well as physical capital in amounts sufficient to assure viability.

II. VERTICAL INTEGRATION [6]

Issues

The study of vertical integration has presented difficulties at both theoretical and policy levels of analysis. Vertical integration has never enjoyed a secure place in value theory because under conventional assumptions it is an anomaly: If the costs of operating competitive markets are zero, "as is usually assumed in our theoretical analysis" (Arrow, 1969, p. 48), why integrate?

Policy interest in vertical integration has been concerned mainly with the possibility that integration can be used strategically to achieve anticompetitive effects. In the absence of a more substantial theoretical foundation, vertical integration, as a public policy matter, is typically regarded as having dubious if not outright antisocial properties. Technological interdependencies (as in flow process operations) or, possibly, observational economies, constitute the principal exceptions.

There is, nevertheless, a distinct unease over the argument. This is attributable, probably, to a suspicion that the firm is more than a simple efficiency instrument, in the usual scale economies and efficient factor proportions senses of the term, but also possesses coordinating potential that sometimes transcends that of the market. It is the burden of the present argument that this suspicion is warranted.

Evaluation

That product markets have remarkable coordinating properties is, among economists at least, a secure proposition. That product markets are subject to failure in various respects and that internal organization may be substituted against the market in these circumstances is, if somewhat less familiar, scarcely novel. A systematic treatment of market failure as it bears on vertical integration, however, has not emerged.

Partly this is attributable to inattention to internal organization: The remarkable properties of firms that distinguish internal from market coordination have been neglected. But the fragmented nature of the market failure literature as it bears on vertical integration has also contributed to this condition; the extensive variety of circumstances in

[6] The argument in this section relies extensively on Williamson (1971).

which "internalization" (the substitution of internal organization for the market) is attractive tends not to be fully appreciated.

The properties of the firm that commend internal organization as a market substitute would appear to fall into three categories: incentives, controls, and what may be referred to broadly as "inherent structural advantages." In an incentive sense, internal organization attenuates the aggressive advocacy that epitomizes arm's length bargaining. Interests, if not perfectly harmonized, are at least free of representations of a narrowly opportunistic sort; in any viable group, of which the firm is one, the range of admissible intraorganizational behavior is bounded by considerations of ostracism. In circumstances, therefore, where protracted bargaining between independent parties to a transaction can otherwise be anticipated, internalization becomes attractive.

Perhaps the most distinctive advantage of the firm, however, is the wider variety and greater sensitivity of control instruments that are available for enforcing intrafirm in comparison with interfirm activities. Not only is the firm able to perform more precise own-performance evaluations (both contemporaneous and *ex post*) than can a buyer, but its reward and penalty instruments (which include selective use of employment, promotion, remuneration, and internal resource allocation processes) are more refined. Moreover, when conflicts develop, the firm possesses a comparatively efficient conflict resolution machinery.

To illustrate, fiat is frequently a more efficient way to settle minor conflicts (say, differences of interpretation) than is haggling or litigation. *Inter*organizational conflict can be settled by fiat only rarely, if at all. For one thing, the parties would have to agree on an impartial arbitrator, an agreement which itself might be costly to secure. Also rules of evidence and procedure would have to be established. If, moreover, the occasion for such interorganizational settlements were to be common, the form of organization converges in effect to vertical integration, with the arbiter becoming a manager in fact if not in name. By contrast, *intra*organizational settlements by fiat are common (Whinston, 1964, pp. 410–14).

The firm may also resort to internalization on account of defects in the prevailing institutional arrangements. The dysfunctional consequences of faulty property rights specifications, for example, may be overcome by common ownership. Also the firm may offer a more efficient communication network.

The firm, however, also experiences genuine limitations in relation to the market. Mainly on account of bounded rationality and greater confidence in the objectivity of market exchange in comparison with bureaucratic processes, market mediation is generally to be preferred over internal supply in circumstances in which markets may be said to "work well." Therefore the question is, when may markets be expected to display defects—which brings us to the matter of market failure.

This aspect of the argument has been developed at some length elsewhere.[7] It reduces to the following series of propositions: the substitution of internal organization for product market exchange becomes relatively more attractive (1) as contractual incompleteness risks become great, (2) as the risks of strategic misrepresentation in interfirm transactions increase, and (3) where market exchange suffers from what may be referred to as "intrinsic inefficiency," especially as this bears on the convergence of expectations. Small numbers of traders, product complexity, and technical and market uncertainties exacerbate these conditions and thereby encourage the internalization of transactions.

Typically, the conclusion of the conventional analysis of vertical integration—which focuses principally on market power considerations—is that, but for flow process operations where materials handling economies are said to be available, the sources of cost saving from integration are "unclear." Transactional analysis, by contrast, reveals that vertical integration may permit the realization of transactional economies over a much wider class of activities. The critical point, as a policy matter, is that in consideration of the variety of circumstances in which product market failures can occur and the potentially attractive properties that internal organization possesses as a market substitute, the a priori case for vertical integration is much more extensive than is commonly realized. If, therefore, contrary to the usual assumptions, vertical integration between successive stages of production often permits real cost savings, its economic consequences in this respect cannot be regarded with indifference. Vertical merger guidelines,[8] which make no apparent allowance for these effects but focus exclusively on the potential anticompetitive consequences of vertical integration, may, accordingly, warrant reconsideration.

Research Opportunities

The argument above, assuming that it is correct, by no means exhausts the issues that vertical integration raises. For one thing, a

[7] The interested reader is referred to Williamson (1971).

[8] See the *Merger Guidelines of the Department of Justice, 1968;* see also Stigler (1968, pp. 302–304).

parallel treatment of the sources and consequences of the failures of internal organization as they relate to vertical integration is needed.[9] In addition, the above argument requires qualification in that it applies strictly to the vertical integration of production. Although much of it may have equal relevance to backward integration into raw materials and forward integration into distribution, I conjecture that the affirmative case for vertical integration may often be less compelling where control over raw materials or distributional channels is involved and that the anticompetitive potential of vertical integration into either of these stages is especially great. A more discriminating approach toward vertical mergers—depending not merely on market shares but also on the stage of economic activity affected and the absolute size of the organization—could easily emerge.

Also relevant to an understanding of vertical integration is the study of intermediate forms of market organization that fall between full integration and arm's length bargaining. Such an investigation may be especially productive in revealing the limits of the firm as an integrating device. The franchise system is of special interest, both in organizational and antitrust terms. What are the incentive and other properties that make it an attractive form of organization? In what types of circumstances does this occur? What contractual limitations (customer, product, territorial, etc.) facilitate efficient exchange and might reasonably be allowed, and when do such limitations have anticompetitive effects? Distinguishing pecuniary price from "full price" [in the sense of Becker (1965)] may be essential for assessing the monopolistic consequences of such restrictions.

The argument could also be brought to bear on historic trends toward vertical integration (including disintegration) in individual industries. Are these developments mainly to be explained by reference to

[9] Of special interest in this connection is the matter of foreclosure. It is often said that vertical integration poses an antitrust problem because nonintegrated firms are foreclosed from securing business that would otherwise be open to competition. Unfavorable market power and unfair competition effects are said to obtain. The economic rationale for these claims has frequently been unclear, however; other students of vertical integration have expressed doubts that foreclosure has any unfavorable economic effects whatsoever. I submit that distinguishing between economic and bureaucratic rationality may help to clarify the issues. Behavior that appears to lack merit, and consequently is dismissed when regarded in economic terms, may not be so bizarre when evaluated as a bureaucratic phenomenon. This distinction between economic and bureaucratic rationality may also be useful in examining other business conduct practices. It is elementary that, where opportunity sets are large, bureaucratic preferences may govern.

technical scale economies and diseconomies [cf. Stigler (1951)], or by the interfirm versus intrafirm *transactional approach* proposed here [and originally advocated by Coase (1937)]? Have recent developments in the study of transactional costs and market failures, together with an emerging appreciation of the properties of firms that commend internal organization as a product market substitute, now made it possible to apply transactional analysis to explain historic trends in vertical integration and related firm and market structures effectively? Put differently, is transactional analysis a research strategy whose time has come?

III. CONGLOMERATE ORGANIZATION

Issues

Industrial organization specialists have been actively concerned with the conglomerate phenomenon at least since Edwards's 1955 treatment of the subject. As Edwards saw it, conglomerate bigness gave rise to monopoly power in subtle but significant ways. Stocking, however, in commenting on the various and diffuse effects described by Edwards, found that most of the alleged anticompetitive consequences could be traced to original monopoly power of a conventional sort. He conceded, nevertheless, that the conglomerate corporation posed significant institutional issues for which conventional theory was inadequate (Stocking, 1955, pp. 358–59).

The dialogue has continued, most recently being a subject for high-level regulatory review in connection with the Merger Guidelines of the Department of Justice, two Presidential Task Force reports dealing with current antitrust problems, and a Federal Trade Commission Staff Report. The emphasis throughout, both in the earlier literature as well as the more recent policy treatments of the issue, has been on the alleged anti-competitive consequences of the conglomerate form of organization.

Such a narrow focus is perhaps appropriate if, as an efficiency matter, the distribution of functions between firms and markets can be regarded with indifference; the principal issues then can be reduced to an application of basic (or extended) monopoly theory to the particular circumstances at hand. If, however, internalization often has significant effects on efficiency, such an approach is arguably too narrow.[10]

---

[10] I have argued elsewhere that organizational innovation, of which the conglomerate is a recent manifestation, often has had (and can be expected to have) remarkable efficiency consequences (Williamson, 1970). The argument, as

Evaluation

Whereas vertical integration involves the substitution of administrative for market processes in response to product market failures, the conglomerate can be regarded mainly as a substitution of internal for market organization in response to failures in the capital market.[11] The capital market has two general functions to perform: funds metering and the supply of incentives, of both reward and penalty types. The extent to which the capital market is engaged in funds metering, however, is severely limited by prevailing retained earnings practices. Baumol concludes from his study of this function that "the stock market is only infrequently given the opportunity to discipline directly the vast majority of the nation's leading corporations" (Baumol, 1965, p. 76). [12] An examination of the incentive properties of the capital market also reveals defects. The external relation that the capital market bears to the firm places it at a serious information disadvantage and thus, because of high imputation costs, limits the efficacy of selective reward procedures. This external relation also prevents the capital market from intervening selectively to correct local conditions. Management displacement, which is an extreme corrective response, incurs significant original and secondary costs.

The conglomerate internalizes both incentive and metering functions. As an internal control mechanism with constitutional authority, expertise, and low-cost access to the requisite data, it is able both to employ additional reward and penalty instruments and to exercise these in selective and preventative ways that are unavailable to an external control agent. As a funds-metering instrument, the conglomerate

it applies to the transformation of the enterprise from a unitary to a multidivisional form at least, is supported by the application of a priori theory to the problems of managing complex, hierarchical, human organizations; by Alfred Chandler, Jr.'s, historical survey of early twentieth century corporate developments (Chandler, 1966); by natural selection considerations; and by a casual review of the conspicuous evidence.

[11] The extent to which this substitution can be expected to be efficacious depends on the internal structure of the firm and the control apparatus employed. The argument here is restricted to divisionalized conglomerate organizations in which strategic decision-making functions (including resource allocation) are assigned to a strong general office and in which a sensitive internal control apparatus has been assembled. For an elaboration, see Williamson (1970).

[12] Also relevant in this connection is the Baumol et al. (1970) article concerning marginal rates of return to alternative sources of funds. The finding that very low rates of return are associated with internal sources of capital reinforces the argument in the text that the funds-metering function of the capital market is incompletely realized.

(ideally) assigns cash flows on the basis of prospective yields instead of allowing them to be retained by the sectors from which they originate. In both these respects, therefore, the conglomerate (potentially at least) [13] can be regarded as a miniature capital market. In the absence, therefore, of countervailing considerations not already reflected in current merger policy toward conglomerates, and assuming that the enforcement of the merger statutes with regard to horizontal and vertical combinations is to remain severe, a more sympathetic attitude toward conglomerate organization would seem to be warranted. Not only are the immediate efficiency gains in funds metering and the supplying of incentives to be valued, but an active market for corporate control (Manne, 1965) is also promoted.

Recent policy proposals concerning conglomerates,[14] however, appear to give no weight to these factors. Based on alleged reciprocity and cross-subsidization dangers together with expressed concern over potential competition effects, enforcement criteria have been tentatively advanced which, if implemented, would relieve several hundred large firms from the forces of competition in the capital market, forces which probably ought to be supported rather than suppressed. Protective efforts by the enforcement agencies to defeat takeover efforts where members of the "business establishment" are the target firms are similarly suspect.[15] Exclusive antitrust concern with competition in the product market (narrowly regarded), to the neglect of competition in the capital market, can result in a perversion of the enforcement process. If, as I have argued elsewhere (1970, pp. 145–50), conglomerate mergers pose genuine public policy issues (in both economic and sociopolitical respects) mainly in a systems sense involving acquisitions by already giant-sized firms, the indicated delimitation of conglomerate merger enforcement is to direct it explicitly toward the giant-sized subset.

Of course not all firms in the giant-sized subset would be affected either by a dominant firm program of the sort suggested in section I or by a tougher policy toward mergers involving giant-sized enterprise. Unless other economic grounds are advanced, therefore, or unless antitrust were to expand its scope to include noneconomic considerations, many giant-sized enterprises would elude the antitrust enforcement net. For those who take the position that antitrust should not be converted into

[13] See the qualifications in Williamson (1970, Chap. 10).
[14] Especially the Neale Task Force Report (1969) and the FTC Staff Study (1969).
[15] For an illustration, see Williamson (1970, pp. 100–102, 171).

an instrument for reconstituting firm size for sociopolitical reasons, such an escape is altogether appropriate. However one comes out on this matter, it is relevant to observe that antitrust is not the only policy instrument that can be brought to bear. The voluntary divestiture programs that some large corporations have recently been observed to engage in are of special interest in this regard.[16]

Some, perhaps many, of these voluntary divestitures have been undertaken in response to pressing cash needs in the face of high interest rates. Others, however, may well have been undertaken out of recognition that large size and proliferating variety eventually result in diseconomies. The parent organization is induced on this account voluntarily to split off some of its operating divisions—either as independent economic entities, as spinoffs (in which some financial interest is retained), or for acquisition by others. This process of "mitosis" represents a variety of organizational self-renewal that warrants a sympathetic public policy response. Not only does it promise operating efficiencies, and on this account alone is to be valued, but it also serves to relieve legitimate sociopolitical concerns over wealth concentration tendencies in the largest corporations.

Research Opportunities

As a research matter, an effort to categorize conglomerate merger activity according to motive and effect is needed. The discussion above emphasizes economic efficiency dimensions of the conglomerate, but it is clearly a more complex phenomenon than that. Many of these issues relate more to tax and securities regulations than to industrial organization per se and might therefore better be pursued by other specialists. A full treatment of the conglomerate phenomenon nevertheless requires that these other factors be assessed.

Of greater interest to industrial organization specialists is the influence of internal structure on performance. Studies of the effects of industry structure on performance are part of the core commitment of industrial organization; cross-sectional studies relating industry structure to performance are common. It is proposed here, however, that the internal structure of the firm (organization form) be introduced as an explanatory variable and that the conglomerate be regarded less as a distinctive organization form itself than as a diversified manifestation of

[16] See *Forbes*, May 15, 1970, pp. 214–20; also *Business Week*, August 15, 1970, pp. 86–87.

either the multidivisional or free-form structure (Williamson, 1970, pp. 142–43, 162).

Although the analysis of organization form itself is at a very primitive stage of development (and, consequently, only the crudest variety of classification scheme exists),[17] it would be interesting to examine the influence of internal structure on performance in the following respects: comparative growth and profit rates among rival firms; marginal rates of return to alternative sources of funds; evidence relating to slack (internal efficiency), perhaps especially in relation to business conditions; evidence relating to internal operating practices, such as cross-subsidization; evidence bearing on "offensive" marketing practices, such as reciprocity.[18] It is probably essential, for the purposes of such studies, to make allowance for firm size effects.

Of related interest is the historical evolution of the multidivision form. Chandler (1966) traces much of this in descriptive terms, but a more formal assessment of this organizational innovation, including its diffusion, would seem indicated. Which firms with what characteristics have been first to employ multidivisionalization in their respective industries, and what factors explain the degree of rapidity with which imitation by rivals has occurred?

An effort to discover the quantitative significance of organizational innovation as it affects aggregate growth rates would be ambitious but not necessarily intractable. What fraction of the residual term in conventional growth models can reasonably be imputed to organizational developments?

Also of interest in this regard is the link between technical and organizational innovation. In what respects have developments of the organizational innovation type altered the locus of technical innovative activity and with what performance consequences? To what extent and in what circumstances does technical innovation take an interorganizational rather than intraorganizational route? Is interfirm exchange—in which different firms with distinctive attributes participate in the inven-

---

[17] The following structural distinctions would seem appropriate from the outset: unitary form, multidivision form, free form, and "other." For a discussion, see Williamson (1970). The need to create additional categories may be evident as the study of internal structure proceeds.

[18] Again, the distinction between economic and bureaucratic rationality referred to in footnote 9 may be useful. There are bureaucratic reasons to expect performance in these respects to vary systematically with organization form, while the conventional theory of the firm is mainly silent on these matters.

tion, development, and final supply stages—really viable? What factors impair its effective operation, and what are the policy implications? [19]

The purpose, locus, frequency, and magnitude of voluntary divestiture efforts need more thoroughly to be documented. Also, consideration ought to be given to means by which to supply incentives that make voluntary divestiture more attractive; this may indeed be the most promising approach to the bigness per se issue. At a minimum, existing tax disincentives to voluntary divestiture ought to be reviewed. Freeing the market for corporate control ought also to be considered as a means by which to encourage very large firms to trim their operations when excessive size and variety are reached; anxious to forestall takeover, otherwise passive firms may be induced voluntarily to exercise restraint. The limits of competition in the capital market in this respect, however, need more fully to be assessed.

The multinational corporation might also be examined in an institutional failures context. To what extent is it a response to alleged imperfections in the capital market? What organizational structures have evolved to support this form of operation, and what limitations (organizational failures) does it experience? What present and potential antitrust problems are posed, and is a corresponding multinational extension of the antitrust enforcement machinery indicated? Even if many of the projections of "world dominance" by multinational corporations are regarded as unrealistic—in that they reflect insufficient appreciation of the limits of internal organization—serious public policy issues may, in individual instances at least, nevertheless be posed.

IV. CONCLUSIONS

It is argued that the study of firm and market structures, and the application of antitrust policy thereto, can benefit from a more systematic examination of the sources and consequences of market failure and by a more thorough assessment of the powers and limits of internal organization. More specifically, product market failure analysis ought to admit to the possibility of default and chance event failures—especially with reference to dominant firm industries. Similarly, the "transactional" limitations that interfirm exchange is subject to warrant explication as these bear on vertical integration. The substitution of internal organization against failures in the capital market, especially as this relates to an

---

[19] For an elaboration of the issues discussed in this paragraph, see Turner and Williamson. Also see Nelson, Peck, and Kalachek (1967).

32 Economic Research: Retrospect and Prospect

assessment of conglomerate organization, likewise deserves attention. The influence of organization form on enterprise performance, and of organizational innovation in general, also merit study. Of particular public policy interest is the possibility of inducing or otherwise supporting voluntary divestiture by giant-sized enterprises.

A survey of the literature on the modern corporation reveals that industrial organization specialists have mainly been bystanders. Partly this is to be explained by the prevailing opinion that the industry, not the firm, is the relevant unit of analysis. But however correct this may be for some purposes, it is less obviously true in others. If one of the most remarkable attributes of American capitalism is its adaptive capacity to invent efficient and viable organization forms in response to changing technological, market, and organizational conditions, to characterize the system in conventional industry terms, to the neglect of internal organization, easily misses much of what accounts for its most significant accomplishments.

REFERENCES

Kenneth J. Arrow (1969). "The Organization of Economic Activity: Issues Pertinent to the Choice of Market versus Nonmarket Allocation." In *The Analysis and Evaluation of Public Expenditures: The PPB System,* Vol. 1. Joint Economic Committee, 91st Cong., 1st sess., Washington, D.C., 1969, pp. 47–64.

W. J. Baumol (1965). *The Stock Market and Economic Efficiency,* New York.

W. J. Baumol, Peggy Heim, B. G. Malkiel, and R. E. Quandt (1970). "Earnings Retention, New Capital, and the Growth of the Firm." *Review of Economics and Statistics,* November, pp. 345–55.

G. S. Becker (1965). "A Theory of the Allocation of Time." *Economic Journal,* September, pp. 493–517.

Yale Brozen (1970). "The Antitrust Task Force Deconcentration Recommendation." *Journal of Law and Economics,* October, pp. 279–92.

A. D. Chandler, Jr. (1966). *Strategy and Structure.* New York.

Ronald H. Coase (1937). "The Nature of the Firm." *Economica,* November. Reprinted in George J. Stigler and Kenneth E. Boulding, eds. *Readings in Price Theory.* Homewood, Ill., 1952, pp. 331–51.

C. D. Edwards (1955). "Conglomerate Bigness as a Source of Power." In *Business Concentration and Price Policy.* Princeton, 1955.

Federal Trade Commission Staff Study (1969). *Economic Report on Corporate Mergers.* Washington, D.C.

Carl Kaysen and D. F. Turner (1959). *Antitrust Policy,* Cambridge, Mass.

Henry G. Manne (1955). "Mergers and the Market for Corporate Control." *Journal of Political Economy,* April, pp. 110–20.

Jacob Marschak (1968). "Economics of Inquiring, Communicating, Deciding." *American Economic Review,* May, pp. 1–18.

Neale Task Force Report (1969). "Report of the White House Task Force on

Antitrust Policy." *BNA Antitrust and Trade Regulation Report,* No. 411, Special Supplement, Part II, May 27, pp. 1–28.

R. R. Nelson, M. J. Peck, and E. D. Kalachek (1967). *Technology, Economic Growth, and Public Policy.* Washington, D.C.

R. A. Posner (1969). "Oligopoly and the Antitrust Laws: A Suggested Approach." *Stanford Law Review,* June, pp. 1562–1606.

———— (1970). "A Statistical Study of Antitrust Enforcement." *Journal of Law and Economics,* October, pp. 365–420.

F. M. Scherer (1970). *Industrial Market Structure and Economic Performance.* Chicago.

G. J. Stigler (1951). "The Division of Labor Is Limited by the Extent of the Market." *Journal of Political Economy,* June, pp. 185–93.

———— (1968). *The Organization of Industry.* Chicago.

G. W. Stocking (1955). "Conglomerate Bigness: Comment." In *Business Concentration and Price Policy.* Princeton, pp. 352–59.

D. F. Turner (1969). "The Scope of Antitrust and Other Economic Regulatory Policies." *Harvard Law Review,* April, pp. 1207–44.

D. F. Turner and O. E. Williamson (forthcoming). "Market Structure in Relation to Technical and Organizational Innovation."

Andrew Whinston (1964). "Price Guides in Decentralized Organizations." In W. W. Cooper, H. J. Leavitt, and M. W. Shelly, II, eds. *New Perspectives in Organization Research.* New York, pp. 405–48.

O. E. Williamson (1970). *Corporate Control and Business Behavior.* Englewood Cliffs, N.J.

———— (1971). "The Vertical Integration of Production: Market Failure Considerations." *American Economic Review,* May.

Issues and Suggestions for the Study of Industrial Organization in a Regime of Rapid Technical Change

Richard R. Nelson
Yale University

My assignment is to consider the treatment of technical change in the industrial organization literature and to discuss how I think the facts and goals of technical advance should impinge on analysis of industrial organization. Since the literature has been surveyed in several recent books, I will concentrate on the second part of my assignment—key issues that require rethinking and research.[1] I shall be concerned particularly with problems in economic theory—the basic conceptual frames that researchers in the industrial organization field have to work with. My remarks will be focused on three main topics: first, the firm as an innovating and adaptive organization; second, the operation of market competition and other (including nonmarket) command and control mechanisms in a dynamic environment; third, some problems of public policy in sectors and situations where technical change is important. In all of these areas I will be crudely summarizing, and anticipating, ideas that Sidney Winter and I are developing.[2]

[1] See for example E. Mansfield, *The Economics of Technological Change,* New York, Norton, 1968; R. Nelson, M. J. Peck, and E. D. Kalachek, *Technology, Economic Growth, and Public Policy,* Washington, Brookings, 1967; and the relevant chapters in F. M. Scherer, *Industrial Market Structure and Economic Performance,* Chicago, Rand McNally, 1970.

[2] Some of the discussion rests heavily on earlier work. See Winter's "Economic Natural Selection and the Theory of the Firm," *Yale Economic Essays,* Spring 1964, and his "Satisficing, Selection, and the Innovating Remnant," *Quarterly Journal of Economics,* forthcoming. See my "Uncertainty, Learning, and the Economics of Parallel R & D Projects," *Review of Economics and Statistics,* November 1959; "A Diffusion Model of International Productivity Differences," *American Economic Review,* December 1968; and Nelson, Peck, and Kalachek, *Technology.*

Note: The author is indebted to M. J. Peck and R. E. Evenson for helpful comments, although they are implicated in no way. Sidney Winter is responsible for the good ideas.

THE FIRM AS AN INNOVATING AND
ADAPTIVE ORGANIZATION

The theory of the firm exists on at least two analytic levels. At the formal level the theory postulates a set of rather simple characteristics of an archetypal firm. The formal theory rests on a deeper body of thought, which I shall call "appreciative" theory, and which attempts to structure qualitative notions about the nature of the firm and its activities in a manner generally less rigorous but richer than at the formal level. The theory of the firm at the simpler, more formal, level has a sharper analytic cutting edge than appreciative theory, and is more capable of generating, or proving, implications. However, the premises and arguments used to specify and justify the formal models rest on appeal to the more basic appreciation of the firm. Further, much of applied research in economics is guided by the appreciative theory at least as much as by the formal theory. This certainly characterizes much of the research in industrial organization. It is my contention that many researchers in the industrial organization field are working with an appreciative theory that is quite different from that underlying our formal textbook models. They recognize this and somehow feel guilty about it.

To put it bluntly, I do not think that the traditional theory of the firm is adequate for analysis of industries in which technical change is important. I think that the appreciative theory of the firm used by industrial organization economists is better than the appreciative theory of the full-time theorist and, further, provides a good basis for formal theory of an interesting and useful sort. The points I will make abut on the long-standing debate about the theory of the firm—behavioralism, managerialism, and so forth—but perhaps even more they are Schumpeterian. I will begin by questioning our traditional theory of the firm at the appreciative level, and then go on to ask some questions about what it is legitimate to assume about firms in the simple, formal models used in the theory of industrial behavior.

In traditional appreciative theory the firm is viewed, first of all, as a *unit;* I will not argue about this point here, but some of my later remarks are strengthened if one recognizes that within the firm there are many people and suborganizations that must somehow be organized. Second, the behavior of the firm is viewed as subjectively rational, in the nontrivial sense that the firm has some objectives in mind and some rather firmly held reasons for doing what it is doing (at one extreme calculations, at the other arguments based on experience). The firm's behavior is viewed as objectively rational in that it would not be trivial for an economist who understands the decision problem to find significantly better policies for the firm than those being chosen.[3] Third, the firm is viewed as being able to operate a variety of technologies reliably and efficiently, subject to the constraint of availability of the necessary inputs (including machinery, skills, etc.). However these constraints are assumed to be not particularly binding over the time period relevant to the analysis. Hence the firm is viewed to a first approximation as being able to employ effectively any technology that any other firm can. I have asserted these elements of appreciative theory in a drastically terse way, while in fact the theory is laden with complexity, nuances, qualifications, and exceptions. I maintain, however, that this is a fair characterization of those aspects of the theory to which we appeal in constructing more formal models.

Once one begins to move from appreciative to formal theory this vision of the firm leads naturally to a model that assumes firms maximize some objective (the deeper theory does not necessarily imply profit) subject to the constraint of a production function and demand and supply equations. Since subjective and objective maximization are the same, the firm can be expected to behave according to the optimizing rules the economic analyst computes. The deeper model almost suggests that all firms are pretty much the same or, rather, provides no reasons why they should be different, and in the absence of special reasons for postulating differences in technological capabilities, access to markets, or of motivation this generally is what we end up assuming

[3] The "subjectively rational" concept means different things to different people, but almost everyone would rule out basically random behavior. Although Alchian and Becker attempt to show that even in this case some of the theorems go through, their proposals do not seem intended as a serious assertion about the nature of firm behavior (Armen Alchian, "Uncertainty, Evolution, and Economic Theory," *Journal of Political Economy,* June 1950; Gary Becker, "Irrational Behavior and Economic Theory," *Journal of Political Economy,* February 1962). At the least some kind of consistency of behavior is expected. And most economists would assume that this consistency is purposeful and is the result of some thought, rather than being purposeless, mindless rigidity (although some use of rule-of-thumb behavior would not be totally excluded). The "objectively rational" point is different, and important. Despite Machlup's earlier insistence that the firm's optimization must be considered as subjective, two things are clear. First, most economists assume that the firm's perception of the world has some contact with reality; firms are viewed as competent—a point I shall develop shortly. Second, in the formal theory the economist plays God, and on the basis of his assessment of what is *objectively* rational, makes predictions as to firm behavior.

in the formal modeling. This is convenient because then we can proceed with the business of modeling industry behavior on the basis of appeal to a typical firm. Later on the theory generates various survival arguments that can be invoked to justify this assumption.

We end up with a theory which views the firm as a competent clerk. This is so both in main-line positive theory and in normative theory. Firms carry out certain well-defined, widely known activities, using generally available resources, picking the activities and their levels according to well-defined, easily computable (and optimum) decision rules. In positive theory this characterization exactly fits competitive theory under the special case where all firms (including the potential entrants) possess the same production sets. It is slightly inaccurate when applied to oligopoly theory where firm differences in production sets, supply conditions, and reaction functions are admitted in some models, or to monopoly where the monopolist is *de facto* unique. But the theory still gives the impression that one set of oligopolists, or one monopolist, is pretty much like any other. In normative theory also the characterization exactly fits the analysis of the optimality properties of competitive equilibrium (with some awkwardness creeping in regarding oligopoly when considering research and development behavior), but the image of the "interchangeable clerk" is strong throughout. This image of the firm stems from our proclivity in our theory to take the technologies, resources, and demands as given. Thus the economic problem is to get the job done efficiently. Bread and automobiles are to be produced in the right quantities and in the right ways given the preferences, resources, and technologies available to the economy. (Let me ignore the question of distribution.) A competitive market provides clear signals as to what is to be done; following the signals is a straightforward business.

This is a plausible characterization of parts of the economic problem and might be a good overall characterization (with appropriate market failure caveats) in a world of no real change; for example, the circular flow world of Chapter I in Schumpeter's *Theory of Economic Development* where "the data which have governed the economic system in the past are familiar, and if they remain unchanged the system will continue in the same way." [4] This is also a world in which a variety of plausible learning mechanisms vitiate the arguments that "tech-

[4] J. Schumpeter, *The Theory of Economic Development,* New York, Oxford Paperback, 1961, p. 81.

nological knowledge is not a public good" and "maximization is difficult if not impossible," and in which Friedman-Alchian evolution-survival arguments seem to make sense (with some important caveats that I will not discuss here).

The circular flow concept, with mechanical, interchangeable firms, probably can keep its footing, if shakily, in a world of smooth, predictable change—such as one with exponentially growing factor supplies and consequent changes in demands. In some models technical change is treated consistently with this view. Indeed, Schumpeter himself, in his *Capitalism, Socialism, and Democracy,* talks about the "routinization of innovation" thus bringing technical change back into his, now dynamized, circular flow model.[5]

However, even if technical change, and adjustment and accommodation to it, can ultimately be routinized, this certainly has not occurred yet.[6] Innovation is inherently creative and personal. In the world of Schumpeter's Chapter III:

> While in the accustomed circular flow every individual can act promptly and rationally because he is sure of his ground and is supported by the conduct, as adjusted to this circular flow, of all other individuals, who in turn expect the accustomed activity from him; he cannot simply do this when he is confronted by a new task.
>
> Carrying out a new plan and acting according to a customary one are things as different as making a road and walking along it.[7]

Economic theory simply has not grasped this distinction. Perhaps the most apparent and striking failure of theory is the proclivity to treat research and development as merely another form of investment, with, perhaps, an unusual amount of uncertainty. But this statement, at the appreciative theory level, just does not characterize adequately the kinds of experimenting, error making, partial correcting, and insightful or blind behavior that seems to go on in major R and D. Nor does it appear to be an adequate general characterization of firms that are trying to do things they have not done before, even though other firms have. Recall

[5] Particularly Chapters 11 and 12.

[6] It would be pedantic to cite many references here. But consider, for example, the case studies in J. Jewkes, D. Sawers, and R. Stillerman, *The Sources of Invention,* New York, St. Martins, 1958; and in J. Marschak, T. Glennan, and R. Summers, *Strategy for R and D,* New York, Springer Verlag, 1967.

[7] Pp. 74 and 85.

Henry J. Kaiser's unsuccessful attempts to master the automobile business.[8] Firms fail, and succeed. Our positive theory at the present time does not seem to have room for the kind of purposive but groping behavior that seems to characterize the operations of firms in a regime of rapid technical change.

Nor does our normative theory adequately deal with this. It is clear that in many important sectors and situations not only is innovation important, but it is an important part of what we want firms to do. To hit this point hard let me shift focus here from the implicit context of private goods and markets to the public sector, and broaden the concept of firm to include organizations of unspecified legal form. In the traditional public finance literature the task of the public bureaucracy, plus contractors, is viewed as analogous to the task of the firm in competitive theory—carrying out activities to provide public goods and, more usually, services. Yet a large share of the important programs are better viewed as efforts to solve problems, where the solution is likely to require new hardware, or a new way of doing things, or a new program, and, hence, "innovation" by the standard definition. Project Apollo is the most striking example. Much of what we are trying to achieve in defense procurement also is hardware innovation. Or, consider the War on Poverty, where what we are mainly trying to do is find, and then implement, programs that will work rather than operating existing programs (which are felt to be unsatisfactory).

I shifted to public sector activity because here it is easier to see that quite often what we are asking the organizations to do is innovate, rather than to meet a well-specified demand in an efficient and well-known way. Yet clearly this also characterizes what we expect and get from firms in a large number of private goods, market-organized sectors. While we hear more than enough about "progress being our most important product," as theorists we have refused to absorb any of this. Robert McNamara's statement is a bit flamboyant ("What in the end is management's most fundamental task? It is to deal with change. Management is the gate through which social, political, economic, and technological change—indeed change in every dimension—is rationally and effectively spread through society" [9]), but we do have to get at least some of this flavor into our theory of the firm.

[8] See "Arrival of Henry Kaiser" and "Kaiser-Frazer, Roughest We Ever Tackled," *Fortune,* July 1951.

[9] Remarks made at Millsaps College, Jackson, Mississippi, February 24, 1967; reprinted in J. J. Servan-Schreiber, *The American Challenge,* New York, Atheneum, 1968, p. 76.

The present main-line appreciative theory has no real room for this dynamic concept, and industrial organization economists long have known intuitively of this deficiency. In an environment of rapid technical change it is implausible to describe behavior in terms of concepts like "subjectively rational"—except perhaps in the trivial sense that the firm is trying to do as well as it can, has some clues as to appropriate behavior, and if it clearly saw ways of doing better would be doing them. But one would expect to find firms often having neither articulate reasons nor appeals to experience to justify what they are doing, and indeed being somewhat nervous about it. It certainly seems inappropriate to view behavior as being objectively rational in any nontrivial sense. In particular there is no case for the assumption that the firm will behave according to the rules the economist calculates as optimal. For obvious reasons it seems a bad misspecification to assume that a firm has access—over the relevant analytical period—to any technology to which any other firm has access. For all of these reasons there is no justification for sliding into the notion of a typical firm in a dynamic environment. Indeed what appears important is that individual firms are unique. In short, the firm cannot be viewed any longer as a competent, easily predictable, interchangeable, clerk working in a well-structured environment on well-defined tasks. Rather, the firm must be viewed as attempting to keep its footing and to make progress in a poorly structured, changing environment by trying and doing appropriate new things.

At the level of appreciative theory, how should we characterize a firm, ideally in a way that is consistent with the traditional perspective where that is appropriate? Let me appeal here to the literature on organizational theory and the behavioral theory of the firm for justification of a presumption that, whether as the result of rational analysis or not, the firm at any time operates according to a set of decision rules that links environmental stimuli to responses by the firm.[10] In the traditional theory it is analytically convenient to denote some aspects of these decision rules as technological, and distinguish these from others which can be characterized as higher-level decision rules. There are some serious difficulties with this clean split, but I will not go into these here. In any case the theory of the firm aims for a convenient, and as simple as possible, characterization of these decision rules. If this can be deduced from, or assumed to be the result of, "maximization" it may be convenient, but it is not necessary to the theory as long as the analyst can

[10] See R. Cyert and J. March, *A Behavioral Theory of the Firm*, Englewood Cliffs, N.J., Prentice-Hall, 1963.

specify the rules somehow. Indeed, a perfectly viable theory would simply declare the existence of these rules and certain aspects of their form, and that they are stable and constant. This really is much of what the maximization theory does. All that the maximization connotation accomplishes is to make the specification plausible.

In the traditional theory these decision rules, both higher order and technological, are viewed as capable of invoking a wide range of firm responses to a considerable domain of environmental stimuli—prices, etc. This is what makes comparative statics work. Let me again appeal to the organizational literature to suggest that, rather, we should assume that the built-in decision rules of a firm apply to only a small domain of environmental conditions and are capable of invoking only a limited range of responses. Put another way the firm at any time commands only a small set of activities and has thought through responses to only a limited range of market contingencies. This, it seems to me, should be an explicit part of the theory.

The model of the firm needs two dynamic components. One is specification of what determines the expansion or contraction of the firm (the level of employment of the decision rules it is using). In other words, the theory needs a submodel of widening investment.

In addition there needs to be an analysis of mechanisms that will induce firms to change their decision rules. The assumption that the firm's decision rules at any time are limited and simple means that in an environment of change, either of external market conditions or of perceived technological possibilities, the firm often will find itself in situations where its built-in rules are, or are felt to be, inappropriate. In our analysis of the process by which firms change their decision rules (perhaps higher order as well as technological) it seems important to be much more sophisticated than we have been about modeling two different, although far from independent, kinds of mechanisms. One essentially is the processes of assessment and search that are largely internal to the firm. An obvious example is research and development, but I also would include operations research, market analysis, management contemplation, etc., where the firm is scrutinizing its own operations and searching for ways to improve them. It seems useful to me to distinguish these internal assessment and search processes from another, undoubtedly linked, class of activities focused on the conduct of other firms. In this latter class the firm is looking to sources of improvement by examining the behavior of other (presumably successful?) firms. While the internal search and the external scan mechanisms clearly should be related at the level of appreciative theory, at the formal level the first class can be viewed as generating innovations (not necessarily improvements); and the second class, diffusion models. While the purpose of these activities is to improve performance I think it would be a grave mistake to assume that they do so reliably. Nor does it seem appropriate to assume that these mechanisms are working all the time on the full range of firm activities and procedures. Indeed, characterizing what things capture the attention of the intelligence mechanism and "turn it on," and the nature of the search process would seem to require theoretical delicacy, and much empirical investigation.[11] Clearly firms differ in these characteristics.

The explicit recognition that many of the decision rules, perhaps particularly the technological ones, are subject to more than very occasional change reduces the attractiveness of a theory that appeals to stable decision rules. I would like to propose, however, that in an environment of rapid change where the lower-order rules may be quite unstable, one might hope to find more stability in the qualitative "meta-rules" that guide changes in the rules. Thus, one might well be able to identify and describe the intelligence mechanism of a firm, its R and D style, and the broad strategy that guides its search for improvements. These surely are more difficult to describe in a simple way than the kinds of rules that have been uncovered on, for example, pricing. But at

[11] One obvious characterization is the "satisficing" model which, in a stylized version, assumes an on-off switch mechanism linked to the performance of the firm relative to its "aspirations" level, and an incremental search starting in the neighborhood of existing practice. Contrary to many complaints about this characterization it certainly does seem a basis for rigorous formal modeling. However, it seems inconsistent with the practice of highly profitable firms to continue to do considerable R and D; it does not adequately model in either the "switch" or the "search" sense the looking to other firms that seems to characterize "diffusion" processes, and it seems unable to account for "major" innovation.

Clearly there are much more sophisticated models of attempted rationality than the simple satisficing model. What is required of theory, I suggest, is that the model not require the decision maker to know more than the model shows he can find out, and that the costs of information gathering and processing be considered at least implicitly. W. Baumol and R. Quandt make some of these points in arguing for the rationality of rules of thumb ("Rules of Thumb and Optimally Imperfect Decisions," *American Economic Review,* March 1964). In several of his works Stigler has generated some very interesting deductions from models that are explicit about the processes by which information and "clues" get acquired. And, of course, J. Marschak has been making some of these points for years ("Theory of an Efficient Several Person Firm," *American Economic Review,* May 1960).

the level of appreciative theory it does seem plausible that firms can be characterized in these dimensions in an illuminating way. Further, it seems plausible that it is at this level that we can find and characterize the sensible response to change characterizations of firm behavior (for example, if wage rates rise significantly, search for ways to cut down use of labor) that we work so hard to deduce from our optimization models. One does not need an optimization model to predict sensible behavior.[12]

Some industrial organization economists, writing about important firms in industries characterized by rapid technological change, have in fact been applying something like this kind of an appreciative theory. They have been digging into and trying to characterize pricing policies and investment rules, without really trying to deduce these from optimization assumptions. Differences among firms have been a matter of some interest to researchers. In some of the literature there have been attempts to characterize the R and D philosophy of a firm or its overall strategy.[13]

Thus the nontraditional appreciative theory apparently meets the test of serving as a useful framework for empirical investigation. However, one cannot rest comfortably with an appreciative theory unless one sees what a formal theory consistent with it would look like. In the first

[12] Note that "neoclassical" implications of a wage increase probably can be deduced even from a simple satisficing switch, incremental search model. The wage rate increase decreases profits which (if they were "normal" before) flips the search switch and improvements will be found on the capital-intensive side of the existing factor mix decision rule. Note that the larger the wage increase the larger the substitution that will be generated (under plausible assumpions) before target profit levels are again achieved.

Note also an "asymmetry" (perhaps realistic?) of this mechanism. A fall in the price of capital will not flip the search trigger. A "never completely off" switch assumption seems necessary to assure neoclassical results in this case.

Note also that it will take time before the new equilibrium will be found and, depending on one's specifications, there will be costs of searching and perhaps mistakes. I take it that there is increasing interest among theorists in treating adjustment lags and costs explicitly. By and large the justification has been in terms of expectations or friction. The kind of explicit search model I have been discussing seems richer.

[13] See, for example, Cyert and March, *Behavioral Theory,* Chaps. 7 and 10; and A. Kaplan, J. Dirlam, and R. Lanzellotti, *Pricing in Big Business: A Case Approach,* Washington, Brookings, 1958. On the question of corporate strategy see Alfred Chandler, *Strategy and Structure,* Garden City, New York, Doubleday-Anchor, 1962; and Neil Chamberlain, *Enterprise and Environment,* New York, McGraw-Hill, 1968.

place, while appreciative theory is inherently somewhat fuzzy, having and working with a formal theory serves to keep the fuzziness within bounds, and to sharpen the appreciative theory. Second, as will be elaborated shortly, the theory of the firm is mainly used as a component of the theory of industrial behavior, in which a more concise, formal, and manipulable model of firm behavior is needed. Thus it seems important to develop a formal theory of the firm consonant with the appreciative theory sketched above.

What is required is a formal theory of firm behavior that is consistent with traditional appreciative theory when appropriate, yet is also capable of modeling the innovative and adaptive firm where that is appropriate. The guidelines are clearly specified in the appreciative theory. The firm at any time should be described by its size and the decision rules it is following. These rules determine whatever endogenous variables the theory aims to explain as a function of a variety of external variables. The firm also needs to be characterized in terms of its expansion and contraction rules and, to anticipate the theory of industrial behavior, the conditions that would trigger entry of a firm that is not in the industry should be specified. Several models of this sort already exist.[14] However, for a model really capable of generating and responding to technological change, it seems essential to incorporate the two kinds of learning processes discussed above; some kind of an innovating or internal search mechanism for improvement, and some kind of an imitation mechanism whereby what one firm does can induce another firm to do likewise.[15] A variety of specifications might be employed. However, it seems essential that at least the innovation generating mechanism not be specified as objectively rational.[16] The burden of prediction that the system move in an objectively rational direction should rest on specification of the search mechanism, on the diffusion machinery, and on responses to market pressure. It would appear that such a theory can be built, and is capable of generating some interesting and plausible implications. The merit of such a formal theory, as sug-

[14] The most elegant model of this sort is Winter's "Satisficing, Selection, and the Innovating Remnant." But several of the stochastic growth models are similar in many respects. See, for example, E. Mansfield, "Entry, Gibrat's Law, Innovation, and the Growth of Firms," *American Economic Review,* December 1962.

[15] Winter's model does have a simple innovation mechanism.

[16] My insistence on this point is stronger than that we must have room in our model for autogyros and Edsels. It has to do with the whole way we look at the technical change process. I will elaborate what I mean in the last section of this paper.

gested above, is mainly to be found at the level of our theory of the industry, to which I now turn.

DYNAMIC MARKET COMPETITION AND OTHER FORMS OF INNOVATION: GENERATING AND SELECTING ENVIRONMENTS

Economists, particularly industrial organization economists, seldom are interested in the behavior of particular firms, but rather in the behavior of industries or sectors. The sector usually, but not always, comprises a number of firms whose behavior cannot be assumed to be independent. Further, the dimensions of sector behavior in which we are most interested usually involve, in an essential if often summary way, specification of what is going on *outside* the particular group of firms that constitutes the sector. We have a tradition of viewing firms as means, not ends. Thus, in our theory of industrial behavior we are concerned with the way in which demands for the output of the sector get generated, and the extent to which the sector satisfies these demands. We also have an appreciation of general equilibrium considerations even in our partial equilibrium analysis. Thus, we are concerned with the costs of operating the sector at various levels and ways, the extent to which the sector operates to minimize real costs at any level of operation, and the way it balances marginal benefits and costs.

Therefore, in conceptualizing at the industry level we generally employ a greatly stripped down and simplified theory of the firm. In addition to specification of the characteristics of firms, our theory of the industry or sector, at both the appreciative and the formal modeling level, involves specification of the environment within which firms operate. The "market" in traditional theory is a model of such an environment which determines the signals, incentives, and constraints which impinge on firms and thus on their behavior. In the traditional theory the environment is determined by two classes of factors. One is the behavior of the outsiders, particularly those who demand the good or service the firms in the sector can provide, and those who supply inputs which have alternative uses or values. The other is behavior of the internal system taken as a group—the competition that goes on among the individual firms. Thus the market is at once a connecting link between demanders and suppliers of both products and inputs, and a constraint upon the behavior of the insiders, in short, an apparatus of command (through effective demand) and control (through competition). There are many other kinds of command and control structures, such as those that characterize primary education, medicine, or the foreign policy establishment. Now, in speaking of industrial organization, I assume that "organization" refers to the command and control structure and that although we tend to concentrate on markets (just as we have tended to concentrate on firms which aim for a profit) the subject matter of industrial organization in principle includes nonmarket command and control structures and organizations with objectives defined in terms other than profit.

I make these more or less obvious remarks so that we can be clear that the traditional appreciative theory of industrial behavior in a market environment is a special case. In the traditional theory the signaling and incentive generation mechanisms are modeled as well-perceived product demand and factor supply curves. The internal control environment is deduced from the condition that *no* firm can improve its profit conditions. Clearly our modeling of sectors which are not controlled by the market would be somewhat different. However, our analysis of market and nonmarket sectors has been dominated by notions of steady state equilibrium associated with our notions of firms as clerks working in a well-defined and relatively constant environment.[17]

The discussion in the preceding section suggests that this positive theory does not adequately characterize the environment of firms where technical change is rapid. The assumption of a well-perceived demand curve for product or supply curve for input is plausible only if one can describe mechanisms whereby these curves in fact get well perceived. This would seem to imply considerable experience on the part of the firms in the industry in the relevant environment of demand and supply conditions. This clearly cannot be assumed in an environment of rapid change in either demand or supply conditions. In particular, it seems completely implausible in considering the demand for a major innovation. Nor under these conditions does it seem plausible to model the environmental constraints in terms of industry equilibrium for that is not where the action is going on. If the industry or problem we are concerned with looks like one in which we can expect change in the equilibrium conditions that is rapid relative to the speed with which equilibrium is approached, or even in which one doubts that equilibrium (perhaps

---

[17] The various "voting" models clearly are in this spirit. It turns out that in these models very often an equilibrium does not exist. But this analysis—the way the problem is set up—is virtually identical to the setup for analysis of market equilibrium.

constant) will be closely approached during the relevant time interval, one should not play equilibrium games. Rather one has to work with an explicitly dynamic model of firm and industry behavior. The competitive environment of any firm is provided by the others moving toward equilibrium, but not by their presence there.

The problem is not just in positive theory as a framework for description and explanation; it is in normative theory as a framework for evaluating performance. If doing things better is a good part of what we are trying to call forth, the market cannot be conceived of strictly as a mechanism to "control clerks" (which is the image of Langian socialists as well as of neoclassical economists who believe that actually having competition may be easier than getting the decision rules of competition followed in the absence of real competition). Rather the market has to be viewed as a mechanism stimulating new mutation (innovations) and doing a creditable job of somehow discriminating between the good and the bad, spreading the former and killing the latter. Even in an environment where rapid technological change is occurring and is highly valued, this is far from all that we want from a market control system. In addition we want that system to stimulate and enforce the neoclassical virtues of economic efficiency, i.e., achieving an appropriate level of output and a minimum economic cost. But since these are going to be changing over time, here, too, market control must be viewed in terms of stimulating moves in the right direction.[18]

Again let me focus on public sector activity to hammer home the point—as well as to introduce a policy issue that I will treat in the following section. The 1960's marked the burgeoning of interest in systems analysis (or cost-benefit analysis or any of a number of titles) as a tool for governmental decision making. Thinking of the decision maker (the systems analyst? the Cabinet Secretary? the President?) as commanding a bureaucracy under him led to a sharp split between the public finance literature, where demands (decisions) automatically were fulfilled, and the industrial organization literature, where demands had to draw forth responses by impinging on a (market) environment of potential suppliers. As experience has accumulated, the clean lines that once used to exist between industrial organization and public finance have been destroyed. There has been growing appreciation that getting the program

---

[18] I state these hackneyed points here not for novelty value but simply to point out that most of contemporary formal theory continues to ignore them. There are exceptions, William Nordhaus's recent book, for example, *Invention, Growth, and Welfare,* Cambridge, Mass., M.I.T. Press, 1969.

performed (the demand met) required the appropriate responses on the part of a variety of organizations, public and private. It became increasingly apparent that this was no trivial requirement.[19] Getting the education or health industries to do what the federal government wants it to be doing turns out to be extremely hard. Part of the difficulty here is that the federal government is only one of many who are trying to get the system to do what they want. But President after President has found it difficult if not impossible to get the State Department to do what he wanted.[20] The point I am trying to make is that having a well-working command and control structure over a group of firms is no trivial matter and that nonmarket sectors have the same command and control problems as the market sector.

However, note that to a considerable degree where the nonmarket sectors seem to be falling down is in effective adaptation to change—technological and other. The education sector has failed to develop appropriate responses to the rise in teacher salaries which, we had hoped, would generate some effective search for ways to increase the pupil-teacher ratio through increased capital intensity or more efficient techniques of teaching. It has failed abysmally to respond to the changing nature of the demands put upon it, largely learning how to educate poor children with non-middle-class values, but also how to educate bored middle class youngsters and how to operate integrated schools. Similarly the health sector has not learned to respond to rising physicians' salaries and fees, and the changing nature of demands put on it.

The neoclassical allegory does not seem to characterize these and, I suggest, most other important kinds of responses to changing factor prices and demands that we want of an economic sector and get out of some. As stressed in the first section, that allegory implies much more complex decision rules keyed to a richer domain of possible external situations and range of responses than we have any reason to assume. For large changes in, say, relative factor costs or demands, I do not think that we can assume firms have a response already thought through or that they can think through to a response *ex ante* that is subjectively and objectively rational. Rather the response has to be considered as an innovation which may or may not turn out to be really economic or really responsive.

[19] See, for example, the last chapter of Charles Schultze's *Politics and Economics of Public Spending,* Washington, Brookings, 1969.

[20] For a very interesting discussion of bureaucratic versus optimizing behavior see Graham Allison's "Conceptual Models and the Cuba Missile Crisis," *American Political Science Review,* September 1969.

Some evidence on this and some implications for the theory of markets and other forms of command and control structures are provided by what has happened to the perception of systems analysis over the past few years, particularly in domestic programs. I think it fair to say that in the mid-1960's there was a faith that with good analysis we could reliably choose *ex ante* among alternative programs on the basis of data gathered and analysis done, even though these programs were in large part untried and the demands had never before been adequately met. We felt we could do this without actually really observing the alternatives in action. In effect the faith here was closely analogous to the economic theorist's allegory about the wide range of choices and circumstances over which the firm can make rational choices *ex ante*. As experience accumulated it became clearer and clearer that there seldom was sufficient information *ex ante* to make reliable bets, and that at the least *ex ante* analysis had to be complemented by *ex post* evaluations. More recently of course thinking about rational policy development has moved more and more toward conscious experimentalism, with the role of the analyst seen as that of setting up a number of experimental programs to obtain data and to try them out, and then on the basis of later data generated in the course of the program, selecting or modifying the menu of alternatives.[21] In short, the model of how public programs should be chosen has moved from the rational choice *ex ante* paradigm to a paradigm which explicitly recognizes that the problem is that of trying out new things, and getting appropriate feedback for screening and selection.

There is no reason to believe the situation is much different in market sectors. While public sector industries seem to have unusual difficulties in selecting and spreading good innovations, in the private sector as well as the public it seems necessary to characterize dynamic processes and mechanisms of selection and diffusion in terms of a flow of innovations, many of which are no improvement at all. Traditional theory that relies heavily on equilibrium concepts seems to abstract from these phenomena and their implications. A good dynamic industry model, I suggest, incorporates a stripped down version of the theory of the firm proposed in the preceding sections. Many people have granted that a quasi-behavioral model is appealing as a model of a particular firm but

[21] For an interesting essay in advocacy see D. Campbell, "Reforms as Experiments," *American Psychologist,* April 1969. For a discussion on the context of the negative income tax see the articles by G. H. Orcutt and A. L. Orcutt, and by G. H. Orcutt, H. W. Watts, and J. B. Edwards in *American Economic Review,* September 1968.

have doubted whether it can be incorporated into an industry model. The claim here is that it can, indeed it is the natural model of the firm to use in a model which includes the possibility of dynamic competition. Firms are characterized by their technologies and static decision rules, and also by the way they generate innovations, expand or contract as a function of their profitability, and imitate (successful) innovations of others. What are the required components of a theory of command and control structure (competition) in an environment where rapid technological change is desired or occurring? The objective is to model demands and competitive pressures in a way that fits our proposed general model, that is consonant with traditional theory where that is appropriate, but which also characterizes more adequately a dynamic, changing environment where that is appropriate.

First, there has to be much more sophistication in modeling the demand for innovation. There are significant problems in positive modeling. It cannot simply be assumed that there is a well-perceived demand curve. One has to get a realistic specification of the speed with which consumers assess the plusses and minuses of the new innovation and of how, in turn, this affects the signals and profitability of the innovating firm. There also are some major normative issues. In a dynamic environment it is doubtful that consumers immediately assess accurately the properties of the new products—there are real issues to be considered regarding the effectiveness of consumer evaluation procedures. While economists increasingly are looking at problems of externalities, these would appear to warrant even more consideration in an environment where rapid change is occurring. There may be something to the argument that with enough time, forces of self-interest will cope with the externalities problem. However, the mechanisms that get externalities reflected in bargains and in incentives to producers cannot be assumed to work quickly. One would expect externalities to be rampant in an environment of rapid technical change.

Second, the dynamics of interactive behavior of the group of firms in the sector needs to be modeled quite carefully. The analysis needs to trace through the manner in which the responses of consumers to an innovation, and of the innovating firm to the success of its innovation, change the environment for other firms and in turn affect their behavior, which feeds back, etc.[22] The nature of the expansion and contraction

[22] For an interesting approach to certain aspects of this, but within a maximization context, see F. M. Scherer, "Research and Development Resource Allocation Under Rivalry," *Quarterly Journal of Economics,* August 1967.

and entry-and-exit behavior of the firms clearly is an important charac-
teristic of the dynamic sector environment. In addition to asking the
extent to which improved performance gets reflected in higher profit, one
must ask how sensitive are expansion and contraction rates to profitability (using the term as a general proxy for whatever the organization
aims for)? How sensitive are entry rates to the average profitability of
established firms? Are there limits on firm size or (more saliently) on the
extent to which particular firms can and will use a particular technology
or innovation? To the extent that expansion rates are not particularly
sensitive to profit or if there are sharp limits on ultimate size, the
efficiency of dynamic response is deterred directly and, also, indirectly
because (under plausible models) less pressure is put on the noninno-
vators. One is tempted to conjecture that sectors in which individual
organizations are bounded geographically (schools?) provide a less
dynamically stimulating environment than those in which growth of any
particular organization is not closely bounded. On the other hand, if
expansion mechanisms work quickly and powerfully and imitation
mechanisms sluggishly, a successful innovator will become a monopolist.
In any case it would seem that analysis of this kind of question is important in studies of any particular sector.

Successful innovations spread in part through growth of the innovators, in part through imitation. It is apparent that in market sectors
both mechanisms are at work, although the relative importance of each
does not appear to have been studied much and probably varies from
sector to sector. It is important to note that the two mechanisms are
not independent. In public or nonprofit sectors the "expansion of the
innovator" mechanism is largely or totally scotched. This means that a
desirable innovation cannot be spread without imitation. At the same
time it means that little or no spur is put to organizations to adopt innovations; there is no-build-up of competitive pressure on the public
monopoly.

There are some compensating considerations. In particular, while
the incentive to imitate is weakened when the innovating unit cannot or
will not expand, at the same time there is under these circumstances
no incentive for the innovators to try to deter imitation (in the private
sector, for example, deterrence is the function of the patent system).
Organizations that cannot expand, and that know others cannot either,
have little to gain by preventing others from adopting their own successful practices. Much of the still remaining faith in the ability to diffuse
successful innovations through publicly structured sectors, despite the

lack of any clear-cut profitlike incentive and despite the existence of sharp boundaries on organizational size, rests on a faith in the apparatus for generating imitation. However, we know precious little about diffusion mechanisms, and patterns of a sector should be a prime topic for investigation in studies of industrial organization in an environment of change.[23]

If one can assume that the speed of consumer response and strength of feedback to suppliers for better or lower-priced products is great enough, that expansion and contraction rules are sensitive enough to profit, and that imitation mechanisms work quickly and reliably relative to the pace at which innovations occur, then it seems reasonable to model the environment in terms of equilibrium conditions. But in a world of rapid innovation, one must pay explicit attention to the transients.[24] It does seem possible to develop a general model that is capable of generating competition either in the neoclassical sense or as Schumpeter described it, depending on what one assumes about key parameter values; and which kind of competition it is in any particular sector clearly makes a difference, both in terms of positive description and analysis, and in terms of the major public policy issues to watch out for.

POLICY ISSUES

In this concluding section I will discuss, in summary form, two major policy issues involving industrial organization in a regime of actual, or desired, rapid technological change. These are worth discussing not only for their own sake, but also for the opportunity they afford to develop further in a concrete setting some of the points made abstractly in the preceding two sections. The first involves issues that arise in trying to program very rapid technological advance in particular sectors. The second involves problems of generating, selecting, and diffusing innovation in public sector or mixed industries.

[23] There have been several first-rate economic studies. See, for example, the several chapters on diffusion in E. Mansfield, *Industrial Research and Technological Innovation,* New York, Norton, 1968. However, there has been very little solid work on "mechanisms."

[24] Obviously this is one of Herbert Simon's central points in his "Theories of Decision Making in Economics and Behavioral Science," *American Economic Review,* June 1959, and in many of the other papers he has written in criticism of the maximization theory.

Programing of Rapid Technological Advance

As remarked earlier, in *Capitalism, Socialism, and Democracy* Schumpeter presented the vision of a future world in which major innovation was routinized. In his *New Industrial State* Galbraith suggests that this stage essentially now has been reached in the large American corporations, and Servan-Schreiber takes a similar position regarding practice in the United States as a whole. The economist's standard model incorporating R and D likewise is consonant with this perception, treating R and D as basically an investment decision not unlike most others.

The theoretical restructuring proposed in the preceding section conflicts strongly with this point of view. In several places I insisted that the innovation process not be modeled as objectively rational either in the sense that outcomes can be closely predicted in advance or in the sense that outside experts (the economists?) would agree on the predictions. In this connection, I insisted that a good fraction of innovations are not improvements. In the industry modeling of technical change I rested considerable weight on the generation of a variety of innovations and hence on processes of *ex post* evaluation and selection.

This disagreement about the nature of the innovation process is important not only for modeling but also for policy. If one believes in the theory of the routinization of innovation—R and D as investment— then one soon is drawn toward looking to R and D, focused on particular national problems, as not just a promising but a reliable instrument for public policy. Further, belief in the reliability of the instrument naturally leads one to analyze in advance the range of alternatives, pick the one that looks best, and put his chips on it. If, on the other hand, one believes that R and D is extremely uncertain, one adopts a "let a thousand flowers bloom" point of view, sees R and D as an interesting, perhaps highly promising, policy instrument, but does not treat the instrument as reliable and, hence, hedges both by using other instruments and by spreading the R and D bets. The first approach leads to the Defense Department style of R and D, and to such forced-paced programs as the supersonic transport and the breeder reactor of the Atomic Energy Commission. The second perception leads one, in public sectors, to spreading of funds, such as is done by the National Institutes of Health, and in private sectors, to seeking to encourage a diversity of research and development, private as well as public.[25]

[25] Clearly, the discussion here harks back to the earlier work done by Burton Klein and others on military R and D. See his articles and also A. W. Marshall

The mutation-selection model seems much more consonant with history. One of the most striking impressions of the history of technological advance in most American industries is the diversity of sources. New products, processes, inputs, and equipment for an industry have come from many different firms in the industry, suppliers, purchasers, new entrants to the industry, outside individual inventors. Many developments that early seemed very promising did not pan out. Many important breakthroughs were relatively unexpected and were not supported by the experts in the field. While detailed histories are not plentiful, and many of these do not shed light on the question, one has the impression that in most of the technically progressive industries, like chemicals and electronics, most of the bad bets were rather quickly abandoned, particularly if someone else was coming up with a better solution, and good ideas generally could proceed along a variety of paths to get their case heard.

The military research and development programs since the mid-1950's, the civilian reactor program of the Atomic Energy Commission, and experience to date with the supersonic transport, are a sad contrast. In these areas the early batting average has been dismal, just as it has been in the domain of decentralized development. But there has been a proclivity to stick with the game plan, despite mounting evidence that it is not a good one. In areas where R and D was more decentralized and competitive, such persistence appears only in exceptional cases. The case of Convair throwing good money after bad on the 880 development rightly is regarded as an aberration, and the fact that General Dynamics had learned its style in military R and D undoubtedly was a contributing factor. But this kind of occurrence is the rule, not the exception, in military R and D. The B-58 and TFX were pushed all the way through development despite mounting unfavorable evidence. The B-70 and Skybolt were halted short of procurement but long after the signals were clear that they were bad ideas. It is a good bet that Boeing would not have persisted so long in pushing its swing wing SST design had the bulk of the funds been its own and had it the expectations of a market test against alternatives. I think the signals are clear enough that the

and W. H. Meckling, "Predictability of the Costs, Time, and Success of Development," and the Comment by F. M. Scherer on Klein's "The Decision Making Problem in Development," in *The Rate and Direction of Inventive Activity: Economic and Social Factors,* Universities-NBER Conference Series, Vol. 13, Princeton University Press for NBER, 1962. For a formalization, see my "Uncertainty, Learning, and the Economics of Parallel R & D Projects," *Review of Economics and Statistics,* November 1959. The discussion below is heavily compressed from a forthcoming paper by George Eads and myself.

present design is in trouble. It is the monopoly position and lack of pressure from an alternative that carries the project forward in its present conception. Similarly, throughout the history of the AEC's power reactor program, there have been complaints that the AEC was persisting in R and D on designs long after evidence had accumulated that this was not an attractive route, and conversely, that the AEC has been very sticky about initiating work on new concepts.

The problem transcends the likely inefficiency and high cost of innovation in industries where the mutation-selection model is not applied. These sectors are likely to end up with a far too limited range of choice and, further, with the government as a powerful lobbyist for the particular technologies. It is rather surprising that the producers of coal and oil, and of power-generating equipment using conventional fuels, have not raised more noise than they have regarding the pressure being applied to the utilities by the AEC to install nuclear rather than conventional power. The evidence on the nature of thermal pollution and nuclear waste problems now is far from clear. Even if it turns out that these problems are more amenable to solution than the pollution and waste problems created by the use of conventional fuels, nevertheless, I think we should feel some discomfort that a strong government lobby has a stake in the issue. There has been more vocal concern about the implications of a governmental financial stake in the SST, perhaps because of the explicit revenue-sharing provisions in the program. But even without a financial stake, the higher executives and congressmen who support the programs have a personal credibility stake in the success of the products and processes they push so hard. It is fairly clear that the success of the SST program, measured in almost any dimension that has been talked about, will depend greatly on the fare structure as allowed and encouraged by the Civil Aeronautics Board. The CAB can go a long way toward making the SST program a financial success by fighting for high fares (to cover the higher cost of the SST relative to the jumbo jets) and uniform fares (so that the lower-cost technology will not be able to compete in the dimension where it is strongest). These are the kinds of consequences one runs into, I suggest, when one tries to predict and plan innovation closely, rather than viewing the innovation process as one of mutation and selection.

The Problem of Achieving Dynamic Efficiency in the Public Sector

Earlier I made the point that the problem of efficiency in public sector activities is, in good part, a problem of industrial organization.

We economists have neglected this perspective before because we have been inattentive to the way that public goods or services are provided. Implicitly we have assumed that once the public decision was made (we spent a lot of attention on how that should be done) it was as good as effected. It now is clear that the public decision (even assuming there is such a clean-cut thing) has to be treated like a "demand" in the theory of industrial behavior, for the appropriate actions usually must be drawn forth from institutions—often some private as well as public—who cannot be assumed to jump simply because the President or a Cabinet Secretary says to jump; and very often the institutional structure provides the President or the public with limited alternative sources or with none; there is no real competitive mechanism.

The combination of the demand characteristics of public sector activities and the organizational structure of the sector apparently yield serious problems in a dynamic environment. I think most of us would agree that the dynamic performance of too large a fraction of the public and nonpublic sector has been extremely poor. While I have not collected any numbers and don't even know what numbers I should collect, my impression is that the average public sector batting average is much worse than the performance, on average, of sectors where the command and control mechanism is based on a real market for final products which links consumer satisfaction rather tightly to the profit or other success measures of the firms.

The problem is not characterized by inadequate research and development (although in some sectors, for example, education or urban services, this may be the case). In both defense and health there has been a lot of R and D, and technical change has been extremely rapid; but it also has been extremely expensive and poorly screened. My remarks above on the proclivity for expensive failures in defense research and development apply. In health one has the strong impression that one of the reasons for rising health costs has been the proclivity of doctors and hospitals to adopt almost any plausible new thing—drugs, surgical methods, equipment—that increases capability in any dimension (and some for which even that isn't clear) without regard to cost.

The basic problem appears to reside in the screening and spreading mechanism and seems inherent in a sector where for a variety of reasons full-blown consumer sovereignty is not possible or desirable and it is difficult to specify a set of clear-cut performance measures on which people can agree. Most of the traditional discussion, however, has been concerned with the characteristics of equilibrium positions. I would like to argue that if the world is like Schumpeter's circular flow, one can conceive of a variety of mechanisms that ultimately can move the decision rules of a public or nonprofit firm toward those which reflect the public interest. The adjustment process clearly would be slow but it would get you there. Thus I am arguing that the serious problems of these feedback systems arise in a dynamic environment where change is occurring or is demanded.

How do we go about improving the performance of our educational system? The answer is not clear. Evidently we want to get more new approaches and programs tried out and evaluated. It seems plausible that the design and funding of major experiments should be undertaken at the federal level. But how does one really "evaluate"? Should success or failure be judged on the basis of how well children or their parents like the program? We long have been leary of putting too much weight on this for a variety of reasons. What objective scores are relevant? Clearly this is arguable. I maintain that with enough time and experimentation with a fixed number of alternatives, and easy modifications, it would be possible to get widespread agreement. But, I repeat, this takes time, and by the time we know how to evaluate the last block of alternatives we are faced with a new block of alternatives and conditions.

This point is salient in considering the new federal ventures toward educational reform. The nation clearly is beginning to put together the apparatus for running a lot of experiments, which seems to me an advance in how to generate an interesting spectrum of innovations. Two other proposed new departures recognize the problem of command and control over autonomous units, and cut at it from antithetical points of view. The educational voucher idea tries to build up the power of consumer sovereignty, and suffers from the variety of worries (alluded to above) we have about this. The performance contracting route attempts to increase the motivating power of those who think they can set objective standards, and indirectly to increase incentives to imitate the experimental programs that score well by these standards. However, the difficulties discussed above remain. As an in-between version one might well think of a voucher system, complemented by widely publicized evaluation of schools' performances, carried out according to the proposed relevant measures and intended to educate and inform parents. All of these are important structural changes. They clearly will help to make the system more responsive and progressive if we can solve the problem of evaluation, of distinguishing good departures from poor ones. But the "if" is basic, and the solution to this is not going to be easy.

These remarks were focused on education so that they would be specific, but I suggest they are applicable to a wide range of public and nonprofit sectors. I make them not because I have a solution, but rather in the hope that the appreciative theory of the problem may be useful, and because I think it extremely important that more economists be working on these problems.

Industrial Organization: A Proposal for Research

R. H. Coase
University of Chicago

It is somewhat of an embarrassment to present a paper on the subject of industrial organization at a meeting sponsored by the National Bureau to celebrate its fifty years of service to the economics profession, and to the public at large. That the National Bureau has had an extraordinary— and beneficial—impact on our thinking and work in many areas of economics is something which cannot be disputed. But, and this is the source of my embarrassment, the National Bureau has carried out very little research directly concerned with problems of industrial organization. I should find it difficult to know how to proceed with this paper were it not that I believe that, in the future, the National Bureau ought to conduct much more research in the field of industrial organization. Indeed, it is just the kind of research which the National Bureau handles in so masterly a fashion: the careful collection of detailed information and its assembly to reveal the patterns of economic behavior, which seems to me essential if ever we are to make progress in understanding the forces which determine the organization of industry. So, if I have very little to say about the work of the National Bureau in the past, I am hopeful that what I (and others) have to say on this occasion will result in the National Bureau's conducting such an extensive program of research that those of you who are fortunate enough to attend the centenary celebrations will hear the National Bureau praised by the speakers for its achievements in the field, not of business cycles, but of industrial organization.

This neglect of industrial organization by the National Bureau is not a peculiarity of its own. It is, in large part, a reflection of what has been happening in economic research generally. Very little work is done on the subject of industrial organization at the present time, as I see the subject, since what is commonly dealt with under this heading tells us almost nothing about the organization of industry. You may remember the occasion on which Sherlock Holmes drew Dr. Watson's attention to the "curious incident of the dog in the nighttime." This brought the comment from Watson: "The dog did nothing in the nighttime." Holmes then remarked: "That was the curious incident." I could not help recalling this conversation when contemplating the present state of the subject of industrial organization.

What is curious about the treatment of the problems of industrial organization in economics is that it does not now exist. We all know what is meant by the organization of industry. It describes the way in which the activities undertaken within the economic system are divided up between firms. As we know, some firms embrace many different activities; while for others, the range is narrowly circumscribed. Some firms are large; others, small. Some firms are vertically integrated; others are not. This is the organization of industry or—as it used to be called—the structure of industry. What one would expect to learn from a study of industrial organization would be how industry is organized now, and how this differs from what it was in earlier periods; what forces were operative in bringing about this organization of industry, and how these forces have been changing over time; what the effects would be of proposals to change, through legal action of various kinds, the forms of industrial organization. Such a subject, solidly buttressed by the kind of research the National Bureau does so well, would enable us to appraise the worth of actions, and proposals for action, which have as their aim a modification of the way in which industry is organized.

This description of the organization of industry, which reflects the traditional view of the subject, is however almost certainly too narrow a conception of its scope. Firms are not the only organizations which undertake economic activities. Apart from associations of various sorts and nonprofit organizations (which may, however, be regarded as special kinds of firm), there are also a large number of governmental agencies which undertake economic activities—many of them of great importance. Almost all, if not indeed all, of these economic activities of government —whether it be police protection, garbage collection, the provision of utility services, education or hospitals—are also provided by firms (or other analogous institutions). It should surely be part of the task of studies on industrial organization to describe the economic activities which are performed by governmental agencies, and to explain why the carrying out of these economic activities is divided up between private organizations and governments in the way that it is.[1]

---

[1] I should like to refer here to an unpublished paper by Victor Fuchs, "Some Notes Toward a Theory of the Organization of Production," which examines this question and makes clear its significance.

Let us now look at how the subject is treated today. I will take as examples two of the most respected books on the subject: Stigler's *Organization of Industry* and Bain's *Industrial Organization*. Stigler has this to say in his first chapter: "Let us start this volume on a higher plane of candor than it will always maintain: there is no such subject as industrial organization. The courses taught under this heading have for their purpose the understanding of the structure and behavior of the industries (goods and service producers) of an economy. These courses deal with the size structure of firms (one or many, 'concentrated' or not), the causes (above all the economies of scale) of this size structure, the effects of concentration on competition, the effects of competition upon prices, investment, innovation, and so on. But this is precisely the content of economic theory—price or resource allocation theory, now often given the unfelicitous name of microeconomics." As to why there are industrial organization courses in addition to those on economic theory, Stigler gives two reasons. The first is that theory courses are very formal in character and cannot go into studies of the empirical measurement of cost curves, concentration, and so forth. The second is that theory courses cannot go into public policy questions, particularly antitrust and regulation; and, as Stigler phrases it, "the course on industrial organization takes on these chores." [2]

Bain tells us that his book's general subject is "the organization and operation of the enterprise sector of a capitalist economy." He describes his approach as "external and behavioristic." He is concerned with "the environmental settings within which enterprises operate and in how they behave in their settings as producers, sellers and buyers." He gives "major emphasis to the relative incidence of competitive and monopolistic tendencies in various industries or markets." [3] What Bain produces is essentially a special sort of price-theory book, dealing with such questions as the effects of concentration and the significance of these supposed effects for antitrust policy. Bain suggests that an interest in what the firm does (its internal operations) is in some sense related to management science, and seems to link this with teaching how businesses ought to be run,[4] although it seems to me that the question could be studied without any such aim in mind. Bain's view of the subject (although not, of course, the way he handles it) is not essen-

[2] George J. Stigler, *The Organization of Industry,* Homewood, Ill., Richard D. Irwin, Inc., 1968, p. 1.

[3] See Joe S. Bain, *Industrial Organization,* New York, John Wiley and Sons, Inc., 1968, p. vii.

[4] *Ibid.*

tially different from that of Stigler. Essentially, both Stigler and Bain consider the subject of industrial organization as applied price-theory. Caves, in his book, *American Industry: Structure, Conduct, Performance,* is even more explicit: "The subject of 'industrial organization' applies the economist's models of price theory to the industries in the world around us." [5]

Industrial organization has become the study of the pricing and output policies of firms, especially in oligopolistic situations (often called a study of market structure, although it has nothing to do with how markets function). It has not helped, of course, that there is no theory of oligopoly or, what comes to the same thing, that there are too many theories of oligopoly. But leaving this problem aside—and without intending to suggest that the questions tackled are unimportant—it is clear that modern economists writing on industrial organization have taken a very narrow view of the scope of their subject.

Now, this was not always the case. If you go to a library, you will find shelves of books written in the 1920's and 1930's dealing in detail with the organization of particular industries. And there was a good deal of more general literature (particularly in the United States) dealing with the problems of what was termed integration, both horizontal and vertical. For example, there was the study published in 1924 by Willard Thorp, *The Integration of Industrial Operations.* And in the Cambridge Economics Series in England, there were such general books as D. H. Robertson's *The Control of Industry,* and Austin Robinson's *The Structure of Competitive Industry.* Earlier, of course, there had been Alfred Marshall's *Industry and Trade* (from which many British treatments took their inspiration). These works varied greatly in their range and treatment, from the discussion of workers' councils by Robertson to the historical account of industrial development by Marshall; from the casual empiricism of the English writers to the detailed statistical investigations of Willard Thorp. But they were all characterized by an interest in how industry was organized, in all its richness and complexity.

It was certainly works such as these which gave me my view of the subject of industrial organization. But what was lacking in the literature, or so I thought, was a theory which would enable us to analyze the determinants of the organization of industry. It was this situation which led me to write, in the early 1930's, my paper, "The Nature of the

[5] See Richard Caves, *American Industry: Structure, Industry, Performance,* Englewood Cliffs, N.J., Prentice-Hall, Inc., 1967, p. 14.

Firm" [6]—an article much cited and little used. This nonuse is not altogether surprising, since the problems that the theory was intended to illuminate have not been of much interest to economists in recent years. But if we are to tackle the problems of industrial organization seriously, a theory is needed.

What determines what a firm does? To answer this question, it is necessary to understand why a firm exists at all, since this gives us a clue as to the direction in which to look in order to uncover what determines what a firm does. In my day as a student (and perhaps this is still true today), the pricing system was presented as an automatic self-regulating system. In Sir Arthur Salter's words: "The normal economic system works itself." The allocation of resources was coordinated by the pricing system. Put as simply as this, it seemed to me then, and it still does, that this description does not fit at all what happens within the firm. A workman does not move from Department Y to Department X, because the price in X has risen enough relative to the price in Y to make the move worthwhile for him. He moves from Y to X because he is ordered to do so.

As D. H. Robertson picturesquely put it, we find "islands of conscious power in this ocean of unconscious cooperation like lumps of butter coagulating in a pail of buttermilk." Outside the firm, price determines the allocation of resources, and their use is coordinated through a series of exchange transactions on the market. Within the firm, these market transactions are eliminated, and the allocation of resources becomes the result of an administrative decision. Why does the firm assume the burden of the costs of establishing and running this administrative structure, when the allocation of resources could be left to the pricing system? The main reason for this occurring is that there are costs that have to be incurred in using the market, and these costs can be avoided by the use of an administrative structure. If transactions are carried out through the market, there are the costs of discovering what the relevant prices are; there are the costs of negotiating and completing a separate contract for each market transaction; and there are other costs, besides. Of course, the firm is attached to the market, and all contracting is not eliminated. But the owner of a factor of production does not have to make a series of contracts with the owners of the other factors of production with whom he is cooperating within the firm.

[6] *Economica,* New Series, 386 (1937). Reprinted in *Readings in Price Theory,* 331 (1952).

The source of the gain from having a firm is that the operation of a market costs something, and that by forming an organization and allowing the allocation of resources to be determined administratively, these costs are saved. But, of course, the firm has to carry out its task at a lower cost than the cost of carrying out the market transactions it supersedes, because it is always possible to revert to the market if the firm fails to do so. And, of course, for the individual firm, the alternative is some other firm which can take over the task if its costs are lower.

The way in which industry is organized is thus dependent on the relation between the costs of carrying out transactions on the market and the costs of organizing the same operations within that firm which can perform this task at the lowest cost. Furthermore, the costs of organizing an activity within any given firm depends on what other activities it is engaged in. A given set of activities will facilitate the carrying out of some activities, but hinder the performance of others. It is these relationships which determine the actual organization of industry. But having said this, how far ahead are we? We know very little about the cost of conducting transactions on the market or what they depend on; we know next to nothing about the effects on costs of different groupings of activities within firms. About all we know is that the working out of these interrelationships leads to a situation in which viable organizations are small in relation to the economic system of which they are a part.

We are, in fact, appallingly ignorant about the forces which determine the organization of industry. We do, it is true, have some idea of why it is that an increase in the activities organized within the firm tends to produce strains within the administrative structure which raise the costs of organizing additional operations (even if similar to those already undertaken): the rise in cost occurs both because the administrative costs themselves rise, and because those making decisions make more mistakes and fail to allocate resources wisely. This is, more or less, the conventional treatment of the management problem in economics.[7] But as firms expand their functions, it seems to me that they are likely to embrace activities which are more widely scattered geographically, and which are, in other ways, more diverse in character. This, I think, must play its part in limiting the expansion of the firm. This is, in fact, a special case of the effect on costs of the combining of different activities

---

[7] See Oliver E. Williamson, *Corporate Control and Business Behavior,* Chapter 2, "Internal Organization and Limits to Firm Size," Englewood Cliffs, N.J., Prentice-Hall, Inc., 1970, pp. 14–40.

within a single firm—not all of which will be adverse. But the existence of such interrelationships suggests that an efficient distribution of activities between firms would involve particular (and different) groupings of activities within the firms (which is, indeed, what we observe). We would not expect firms to be similar in the range of activities that they embrace; but, so far as I am aware, the distribution of activities between firms is not something on which we have much to say.

Why is it that we seem to have so little to say? In part, it can be explained by the character of the economic analysis which apparently deals with the organization of industry—by which I mean the treatment of the optimum size of the firm and of economies of scale. This analysis, which sounds as if it is dealing with the organization of industry (although it does not), tends to reassure those who might be worried by a more conspicuous gap. It is not difficult to see what is wrong with the theory of the optimum size of firm, as presented in economics. First of all, what is wanted is not a statement about *the* optimum size of the firm (presumably with a different optimum for each industry), but a theory which concerns itself with the optimum distribution of activities, or functions, between firms. Second, the theory of the optimum size of the firm is not about the size of the firm, in the sense of dealing with the activities carried out by the firm, but is concerned with the determination of the size of its output. Moreover, even here, current theory is only concerned with the output of particular products, or a generalized product, and not with the range of products produced by the firm. This last statement is somewhat overbold, since economists may also use value of assets or number of employees to measure the size of the firm—but I am, at any rate, correct in saying that there is very little discussion about what firms actually do.

The discussion of economies of scale is largely concerned with the relation of costs to output (the derivation, in effect, of the cost schedule). Such discussion tells us nothing about the effect on costs of conducting one activity, of undertaking another activity, or about the relative costs to different kinds of firms of undertaking particular activities. Still less does it deal with the extent to which there is "contracting out" as the output of a product (or generalized product) is increased. What has happened is that the character of the analysis in which economists have engaged has not seemed to demand an answer to the questions I have been raising.

I would not, however, wish to omit mention of the one paper which does attempt to deal with these questions, namely, Professor

Stigler's article, "The Division of Labor Is Limited by the Extent of the Market." [8] As we all know, this statement of Adam Smith's, although correct (all of Adam Smith's statements are correct), has caused some perplexity, since it did not seem to be consistent with the existence of competitive conditions. In the course of resolving this problem, Professor Stigler discusses the conditions which lead to the emergence of specialized firms, and which influence the extent of vertical integration. Professor Stigler does not take us very far, but he takes us as far as we have gone.

I have said that the character of the analysis used by economists has tended to conceal the fact that certain problems in industrial organization are not being tackled. But I think there is a much more important reason for this neglect: interest in industrial organization has tended to be associated with the study of monopoly, the control of monopoly, and antitrust policy. This is not a recent development. When in the late nineteenth century, economists came to be interested in problems of industrial organization, they were confronted with the problem of the trust in the United States and the cartel in Germany. It was, therefore, natural that with the development of antitrust policy in the United States, interest in antitrust aspects of industrial organization came to dominate the subject.

This has had its good and its bad effects but, in my opinion, the bad by far outweigh the good. It has, no doubt, raised the morale of many scholars working on problems of industrial organization, because they feel that they are engaged on work which has important policy implications. It has had the salutary result of focusing these scholars' attention on real problems concerning the way in which the economic system operates. It has also led them to utilize some sources of information which might otherwise have been neglected. Still, in other respects, the effects seem to me to have been unfortunate. The desire to be of service to one's fellows is, no doubt, a noble motive, but it is not possible to influence policy if you do not give an answer. It has therefore encouraged men to become economic statesmen—men, that is, who provide answers even when there are no answers. This tendency has discouraged a critical questioning of the data and of the worth of the analysis, leading the many able scholars in this field to tolerate standards of evidence and analysis which, I believe, they would otherwise have rejected. This association with policy—and antitrust policy in particular

[8] See George J. Stigler, footnote 2 above, pp. 129–141.

—gave a direction to the study of industrial organization which prevented certain questions from being raised or, at any rate, made it more difficult to do so. The facts as stated in antitrust cases were accepted as correct (or substantially so). The ways in which the problem was viewed by the lawyers (judges and advocates) were accepted as the ways in which we should approach the problem. The opinions of the judges often became the starting point of the analysis, and an attempt was made to make sense of what they had said. This so tangled the discussion that most economists were, apparently, unaware of having failed. It is true that this is beginning to change, as a result of the work of, among others, Adelman and McGee,[9] but the dominant approach is still, I think, as I have stated it.

One important result of this preoccupation with the monopoly problem is that if an economist finds something—a business practice of one sort or other—that he does not understand, he looks for a monopoly explanation. And as in this field we are very ignorant, the number of ununderstandable practices tends to be rather large, and the reliance on a monopoly explanation, frequent. Of course, more recently, the desire to reduce the burden of taxes has become another way of explaining why businesses adopt the practices they do. In fact, the situation is such that if we ever achieved a system of limited government (and, therefore, low taxation) and the economic system were clearly seen to be competitive, we would have no explanation at all for the way in which the activities performed in the economic system are divided between firms. We would be unable to explain why General Motors was not a dominant factor in the coal industry, or why A & P did not manufacture airplanes.

May I give an illustration taken from a recent article in the *Journal of Law and Economics?* The article is by Professor John L. Peterman, "The Clorox Case and the Television Rate Structures." [10] Procter and Gamble acquired Clorox and the merger was challenged under the antitrust laws. A large part of the case against Procter and Gamble was that they were able to obtain discounts for television advertising of the order of 25 to 30 per cent—discounts which were not available to smaller firms. This led many to the conclusion that this was a manifestation of monopoly in the television industry and an example of price discrimina-

[9] See, for example, Morris A. Adelman, "The A and P Case: A Study in Applied Economic Theory," *Quarterly Journal of Economics* (May, 1949), and John S. McGee, "Predatory Price Cutting: The Standard Oil (N.J.) Case," *Journal of Law and Economics* (October, 1958).

[10] *Journal of Law and Economics* (October, 1968), pp. 321–422.

tion. However, a careful study by Professor Peterman showed that the discount structure was, in fact, designed to compensate for the fact that those who purchased advertising time in the way that Procter and Gamble did, obtained, on the average, worse time (time with a smaller audience). In fact, if the amounts paid were related not to time but to the audience size, the advantages which Procter and Gamble were alleged to have, disappeared.

This is, I think, a common situation. There is some unusual feature —in this case, large discounts. The conclusion is immediately drawn: monopoly. What people do not normally do is inquire whether it may not be the case that the practice in question is a necessary element in bringing about a competitive situation. If this were done, I suspect that a good deal of supposed monopoly would disappear, and competitive conditions would be seen to be more common than is now generally believed. In a similar fashion, vertical integration (let us say, a manufacturer acquiring retail outlets) is often thought of as foreclosure, a means of keeping out other manufacturers, rather than as a possibly more efficient method of distribution. Similarly, mergers tend to be thought of as methods of obtaining monopoly, or are related to the business cycle, and the possibility that they may bring economies, although not ignored, tends to receive less attention.

I have given instances of the way in which the association of the study of industrial organization with antitrust policy has created a disposition to search for monopolistic explanations for all business practices whose justification is not obvious to the meanest intelligence. But, surely, you will ask, economists have not confined themselves to the role of camp followers to the judges and the antitrust lawyers in the Department of Justice and the Federal Trade Commission. The answer is that they have not so confined themselves—but it is questionable whether what else they have done has been more useful. During the last twenty years, a major preoccupation of economists working in what is called industrial organization has been the study of concentration in particular industries and its effects. The effects they looked for were monopolistic, and the way they expected them to be manifested was in higher profits. As it seems to me (and I must confess that this is not a field with which I have great familiarity), the results obtained flattered only to deceive. There was a relationship between concentration and profitability, weak it is true, but, we are told, statistically significant. On theoretical grounds, it was rather puzzling. If the elasticity of supply to the industry was high, or the elasticity of demand for its products was high, one would not expect any relation between concentration and profitability. And if fewness of producers is supposed to bring greater profits as a result of collusion, there are many factors other than fewness of numbers which affect the likelihood of successful collusion. So, it was rather strange that there was any detectable relationship at all. There were other puzzling features of the results, such as that the relationship became worse, the more sharply defined the industry. But, perhaps, we should cease worrying over the significance of these concentration studies. I say this because of an article entitled "The Antitrust Task Force Deconcentration Recommendation," which has recently appeared. (It is a critique of a proposal which took the conclusion of these studies seriously and tried to do something about it.) [11] The author, Professor Brozen, claims that the results achieved in these concentration studies reflect disequilibrium conditions in the periods in which the studies were made. If the calculations are reworked for later periods, high profit rates tend to decline, low rates tend to rise. If the results reported by Professor Brozen hold up after the criticism to which they inevitably (and rightly) will be exposed, there can, I think, be little doubt that this article brings an era to an end. The study of concentration and its effects will be in shambles. Should this really turn out to be the position, the present may well be a good time to pick up the pieces and start again.[12] That some rethinking of our theory is called for seems to me clear. But just as important, at the present stage, would be the gathering in a systematic way of new data on the organization of industry so that we can be better aware of what it is that we must explain.

I should now like to return to the undertaking of economic activities by organizations other than firms and, particularly, by governmental organizations. Somewhat surprisingly, this is not a subject with which economists have been much concerned. Insofar as they have considered this topic, it was as part of a discussion of what the government *ought* to do, whether by taxation, regulation, or operation, to improve the working of the economic system; of these three policies, the least attention has been given to government operation. In any case, the discussion had two weaknesses. First, no serious investigation was made of how

[11] *Journal of Law and Economics* (October, 1970), pp. 279–292.

[12] It has been suggested to me that the lack of any significant relationship between concentration and profitability does not imply that there may be a significant relationship between concentration and other aspects of industrial organization. This may well be true. However, I doubt whether we will understand the reasons for these relationships until we make a direct attack on the problem.

the policies advocated would work out in practice. To justify government action, it was enough to show that the "market"—or perhaps more accurately, private enterprise—failed to achieve the optimum. That the results of the government action proposed might also fall short of the optimum was little explored, and in consequence, the conclusions reached have little value for appraising public policy.

The discussion, however, has a further weakness which is more relevant to my main theme here. It seems to have been implicitly assumed that the same considerations which led welfare economists to see the need for govenment action would also motivate those whose active support was required to bring about the political changes necessary to implement these policy recommendations. In this, we are wiser than we were, in large part because of the new "economic theory of politics." We are beginning to perceive the nature of the forces which bring about changes in the law—and there is no necessary relationship between the strength of forces favoring such changes and the gain from such changes as seen by economists. It suggests that economists interested in promoting particular economic policies should investigate the framework of our political system to discover what modifications in it are required if their economic policies are to be adopted, and should count in the cost of these political changes. This presupposes that the relationship between the character of the political institutions and the adoption of a particular economic policy—in our case, government operation of industry—has been discovered. We do not know much about these relationships, but uncovering them seems to me a task to be assumed by students of industrial organization. It is easy to observe that the extent of government participation in industry has varied over time, has varied between industries, and has varied between various geographical areas. I have no doubt that as a result of research on this aspect of industrial organization, the factors which have contributed to these differences will be uncovered. It is my hope that the National Bureau will participate in this work.

I have suggested that what is wanted is a large-scale systematic study of the organization of industry in the United States. I have also suggested that this would yield best results if conducted in an atmosphere in which the scientific spirit is not contaminated by a desire (or felt obligation) to find quick solutions to difficult policy issues. Where else could such conditions of scientific purity be found than in the National Bureau? This proposal for more research is founded on my belief that it is unlikely that we shall see significant advances in our theory of the organization of industry until we know more about what it is that we must explain. An inspired theoretician might do as well without such empirical work, but my own feeling is that the inspiration is most likely to come through the stimulus provided by the patterns, puzzles, and anomalies revealed by systematic data-gathering, particularly when the prime need is to break our existing habits of thought.

I said that the National Bureau had done very little in the field of industrial organization. But the subject has not been completely ignored and, as Professor Stigler has indicated (no doubt correctly), there is much to be learnt about industrial organization in National Bureau studies on finance, taxation, and technological advances.[13] But there are works sponsored by the National Bureau which deal squarely with industrial organization, and I should say something about them. That they are works of high scholarship, dealing with topics of great importance, is not in dispute; but, given the present state of the discipline, it is hardly surprising that these works should have ignored, or touched only lightly upon, certain issues, or that the treatment was, in other respects, incomplete.

The chief works published by the National Bureau on industrial organization would seem to be: Solomon Fabricant, *The Trend of Government Activity in the United States Since 1900;* Ralph L. Nelson, *Merger Movements in American Industry;* and Michael Gort, *Diversification and Integration in American Industry.*

I will first say something about Professor Fabricant's work, since it deals with government activity, an aspect of industrial organization which seems to me to have been somewhat neglected. This book does not confine itself to questions of public finance or regulation, which is important, revealing as it does an interest on the part of the National Bureau in the role of government as an organizer of economic activity. The discussion is, however, largely concerned with analyzing the composition of government employment and expenditures, with relating these to the totals for the economy as a whole, with discovering trends in the aggregates, and with similar questions. Of itself, the study does not throw much light on the factors which cause the government to operate economic enterprises, but it does provide a good deal of data which would be useful in an investigation which had this as its aim. I would hope that in some future study, the National Bureau will collect detailed informa-

[13] See George J. Stigler, Foreword to Michael Gort's book, *Diversification and Integration in American Industry,* New York, National Bureau of Economic Research, 1962, p. xxi.

tion about government operations in such a form that, as a result of analysis, we will discover the factors which cause government operation to be chosen as against other methods of economic organization. In this connection, I would hope that the National Bureau makes a study of government contracting, since the question at issue is not simply one of government versus private enterprise, but also of government operation versus "contracting out" for products and services which the government itself demands.

Next, let us consider the books of Professors Nelson and Gort, which deal with problems of industrial organization of a more traditional kind. Professor Nelson's impressive work is mainly concerned with the development of time series for mergers in the United States; with relating merger movements to business cycles; and with testing, insofar as his data allow this, the main explanations advanced to account for the variations in merger activity. Professor Nelson does not give many details of the kind of organization created by the mergers (the kind of activities that were brought together within the same organization), nor does he deal with what happened after the merger was consummated. As a consequence, we are not able to judge what the role of the various merger movements was in shaping the industrial structure of the United States, or how far they were a response to fundamental changes which required such modifications in organization to promote efficiency. All this, I may add, is recognized by Professor Nelson, who concludes: "The important and interesting job of producing answers remains to be done." [14]

Of the three works that I have mentioned, that by Professor Gort comes closest to what I have in mind when I speak of the research on industrial organization that we need today. Professor Gort does deal with the question of the range of activities organized within the firm, and there can be few problems of importance in industrial organization on which he does not touch. However, Professor Gort abandoned the more straightforward methods of earlier investigators, such as Willard Thorp. He makes the central theme of his book a study of diversification. He measures trends in diversification, and seeks to discover the economic characteristics of diversifying firms, and of the industries entered by diversifying firms. Degrees of diversification are not, however, easy to define or to measure, and the results which Professor Gort presents are

[14] See Ralph L. Nelson, *Merger Movements in American Industry*, New York, National Bureau of Economic Research, 1959, p. 126.

difficult to interpret without knowledge of the underlying industrial structure. An approach to the organization of industry via a study of diversification is not without interest, but it presents a strange first step. It is as if we started an investigation of eating habits by measuring the degree of diversification in the foods consumed by each individual, rather than by discovering what the patterns of food consumption actually are.

In my view, what is wanted in industrial organization is a direct approach to the problem. This would concentrate on what activities firms undertake, and would endeavor to discover the characteristics of the groupings of activities within firms. Which activities tend to be associated and which do not? The answer may well differ for different kinds of firm; for example, for firms of different size, or for those with a different corporate structure, or for firms in different industries. It is not possible to forecast what will prove to be of importance before such an investigation is carried out; which is, of course, why it is needed. In addition to studying what happens within firms, studies should also be made of the contractual arrangements between firms (long-term contracts, leasing, licensing arrangements of various kinds including franchising, and so on), since market arrangements are the alternative to organization within the firm. The study of mergers should be extended so that it becomes an integral part of the main subject. In addition to a study of the effects of the rearrangement of functions between firms through mergers, we also ought to take into account "dismergers" (the breaking up of firms); the transfer of departments or divisions between firms; the taking on of new activities and the abandonment of old activities; and also —which tends to be forgotten—the emergence of new firms.

Studies such as those I have just outlined would bring under review the whole of the organization of industry in the United States, and would put us in a position to start the long and difficult task of discovering what the forces are which shape it. It is my hope that the National Bureau will play a major role in bringing about this renaissance in the study of industrial organization.